From Failure to Success

Everyday Habits and Exercises to Build Mental Resilience and Turn Failures Into Successes

By Martin Meadows

Download Another Book for Free

I want to thank you for buying my book and offer you another book (just as valuable as this one): *Grit: How to Keep Going When You Want to Give Up*, completely free.

Visit the link below to receive it:

http://www.profoundselfimprovement.com/failure

In *Grit*, I'll tell you exactly how to stick to your goals, using proven methods from peak performers and science.

In addition to getting *Grit*, you'll also have an opportunity to get my new books for free, enter giveaways, and receive other valuable emails from me.

Again, here's the link to sign up:

http://www.profoundselfimprovement.com/failure

Table of Contents

Download Another Book for Free 2

Table of Contents 4

Prologue 7

Chapter 1: What Is Your Definition of Failure? 13

PART 1: 7 Types of Failure and How to Handle Them 27

Chapter 2: Dealing With a Failure You Couldn't Prevent 29

Chapter 3: Dealing With a Failure Due to
Unrealistic Expectations 38

Chapter 4: Dealing With a Failure Due to a Lack of Focus 46

Chapter 5: Dealing With a Fear-Driven Failure 51

Chapter 6: Dealing With a Failure Due to Self-Sabotage 62

Chapter 7: Dealing With a Failure Due to Impatience 74

Chapter 8: Dealing With a Failure Due to Self-Licensing 87

PART 2: 5 Rules and Exercises to Develop
and Maintain a Success-Friendly Mindset 96

Chapter 9: You Must Live Your Life the Hard Way
and Regularly Embrace Uncertainty 98

Chapter 10: You Must Show the Middle Finger to Your Ego 105

Chapter 11: You Must Feel Worthy of Success 110

Chapter 12: You Must Take Personal Responsibility 116

Chapter 13: You Must Identify What You Want
— And Go After It 121

PART 3: A 5-Step Process to Cope With Failure
and Bounce Back 127

Chapter 14: Process the Failure 130

Chapter 15: Forgive Yourself 135

Chapter 16: Change Your State 141

Chapter 17: Learn From It 145

Chapter 18: Restart Your Efforts 148

PART 4: Three Master Strategies to Build Strength
to Keep Going 151

Chapter 19: Develop a Passion 153

Chapter 20: Adopt the Experimental Approach 159

Chapter 21: Find Value Regardless of Results 166

PART 5: Four Reasons to Give Up 171

Chapter 22: Give Up If It Isn't Congruent With You 173

Chapter 23: Give Up If You Won't Achieve
the Level of Performance or Achievement You Want 182

Chapter 24: Give Up If You Only Keep Going
Because of Sunk Costs 186

5

Chapter 25: Give Up If You're Constantly Playing Catch-Up 189

Epilogue 192

Download Another Book for Free 194

Could You Help? 195

About Martin Meadows 196

References 198

Prologue

I spent weeks working with my designer to develop a video course about self-discipline. I thought that people would enjoy watching fun, animated graphics to learn about self-discipline and it would become one of my most successful products.

I published the course on the biggest platform for video courses, distributed free coupon codes to hundreds of people and waited for an endless rain of money...

But it didn't happen.

I made a whopping $23.63 in the first month and $51.40 in the second month. Earnings picked up somewhat over the next few months, but considering I had invested a few thousand dollars in my product, I was still well in the red. Most people enjoyed my course, but you can't pay bills with positive feedback.

I decided to invest in a new, shorter course and make numerous improvements. The final product was immensely better than the first course. I also spent almost $1000 less, so I was sure I would recoup my investment quickly.

Except I didn't.

The course completely failed, making a grand total of $368.08 in the first six months of its existence.

I couldn't give up. I knew that I could make this idea work. After all, I *was* making *some* money, just not enough to recoup my investment.

I invested about $5000 in my third course. I provided even more practical and actionable content, and my designer created beautiful new illustrations and engaging animations.

Surely I succeeded *this* time, right?

Not really. I made $250 in the first month, and over the subsequent months, earnings took a dive. I lost almost everything I invested in this course.

As a last attempt, I decided to create a short video course that I would offer completely for free. I thought that if people enjoyed my free course, they would purchase other courses.

No dice.

I invested over $2000 and only recouped $65.21 in YouTube advertising revenue. Even worse, the free course didn't translate into more sales of the paid courses.

I would love to tell you that the story had a happy ending, but it didn't. 13 months have passed since I released my first course and I'm still almost $10,000 in the red.

Even though I'm a bestselling author with thousands of loyal readers, I still failed, big time. I'm telling you this because I want to show you that nobody is immune to failure. I'm just like you. What qualifies me to write a book about struggle are all of the failures I've experienced to this day and the tools I've developed to handle them.

Before, I would torture myself for days, getting angry at everyone and everything, thinking how *unfair* it was for me to fail. Now, to me failure is pretty much like water off a duck's back.

To some people failure is the worst thing in the world, while to others it's exciting and even inspiring.

One person doesn't stop even for a second when they face obstacles or make mistakes, while another person immediately gives up, convinced that success is black or white: you either reach your goal or you don't.

What makes the difference between those people? How can you use failure to propel you to become a better person? What if there were a simple tweak that would help you redefine what failure means to you? Lastly, how can you stop getting so angry and discouraged at failure, accept it with dignity and proclaim: "On to the next one!"?

This book will answer all of these questions with plenty of real-world examples from the realms of personal development, health, fitness, business, relationships, and numerous other domains where failure is a constant companion.

As a guy obsessed with personal development, failure is an inherent part of my life. Over the years, I failed countless times in:

- Business — It took me several long years of struggle to launch my first profitable business. Most of the time, nobody but me believed that I would ever become a successful entrepreneur. And I don't blame them. I failed time after time, constantly riding a wild rollercoaster of getting my hopes up, falling into depression, then launching a new project that was followed by failure and another bout of depression.

- Health and Fitness — It took me years to change certain unhealthy habits and build a fit physique. For years, despite exercising religiously several times a week, if you looked at my body, you'd never think I went to the gym at all. In fact, pretty much every new gym-goer had better results after a couple of months than I did after *years* of exercise, sacrifices, and countless hours spent researching how to turn my fitness around.

- Relationships — For years, my extreme shyness prevented me from having a normal social life. Imagine a guy who radiates total awkwardness when merely talking to a woman about a neutral topic. Yeah, that was me.

- Sports and Learning New Skills — I spent a year learning how to play tennis, only to realize that I was a hopeless case. I spent weeks learning Arabic only to discover that when I visited an Arabic-speaking country, almost nobody wanted to speak Arabic with me, let alone be impressed by my non-existent skills. I tried to learn how to invest in stock options only to realize that I couldn't even understand how fees were calculated.

To say that I'm good buddies with failure would be an understatement. Fortunately, this also means I learned a lot about it. My intention for this book is to help you get more comfortable with struggles and failure and aid you in reaching your goals.

Throughout the book I'll use the word "failure" or "struggle" to define any kind of a negative event that sets you back. Whenever I use these words, please think of them in a broad sense. The concepts don't apply only to failing your diet or an exam. We'll talk about dealing with adversity, handling a crisis, overcoming a failure due to personal deficiencies and bouncing back after making stupid mistakes (I'm a certified expert in this one!).

Each chapter comes with practical concepts and habits you can quickly introduce in your life. Throughout the book you'll also find "Exercise" boxes that suggest additional actions you can take to improve your life and "Empowering Stories," in which you'll learn about people who managed to achieve their goals despite constant struggles, rejection, crises, or failures. Finally, each chapter is summarized with a quick recap covering the most important points.

Before we begin, I need to set the right expectations for you and address some important issues.

Let's start with the big one: I am *not* a qualified therapist and I am *not* some kind of a guru who knows everything there is to know about failure and success. I've simply had my share of those events and decided to share my experience in this book, along with many other tips I learned, thanks to scientific research and lessons from experts in their domains.

According to the paper titled, "Do self-help books help?" by Ad Bergsma, self-help books show "options for thinking and acting from the psychological toolkit of the individual that are underdeveloped or could be used more often."[1] This is how I want you to think about this book: —I present you with some alternative ways of thinking to help you deal with failure and achieve success.

You choose what you want to use in your life based on what you think is best for you. You are your own therapist, and you're fully responsible for your own success.

It's important you have the right expectations about what this book can and cannot do for you. While you'll learn numerous techniques to handle failure, you'll never completely eradicate struggles from your life. It's an inherent condition of our lives as human beings and it's good, because failure can give you as much—if not more—than success. This book is one of the gifts that failure gave me; —if it weren't for the countless mistakes, obstacles and setbacks, I'd have never learned how to develop mental toughness.

While I don't believe that you should continuously and deliberately seek failure, it's a fact of life that you'll always encounter it along the way. Don't you think you might as well befriend it, rather than consider it a mortal enemy? If you agree, let's proceed to the first chapter and talk about the true nature of failure in more detail.

Chapter 1: What Is Your Definition of Failure?

According to the Merriam-Webster dictionary, failure means a lack of success.[2] The logical assumption that follows is that you're only successful when you reach your end goal. In other words, the process doesn't matter. It's spelled out in black or white terms: it's either success or it's failure. This disempowering definition is one of the primary reasons why people fear and despise failure.

You could argue that it's all just semantics, but language shapes your behavior, so it's important to use the right, empowering words. You might consider the following few paragraphs a bit esoteric, but please bear with me and you'll probably start seeing failure in a new light.

If you face a difficult problem and you tell yourself, "I don't know how to deal with it," you'll think of reasons why you can't do it — and not potential solutions. Your brain acts on your instructions, and it's the words you use that steer your thinking process. How likely are you to solve the problem if you're wasting energy coming up with excuses?

If instead you tell yourself, "Okay, let's find a way to figure it out," you'll think of potential solutions and probably solve the problem. Same problem, different words, different outcome.

Let's illustrate this with a quick example:

John and Kate want to start a business. Both come from the same background and have the same exact resources at their disposal.

13

John says: "If only I had money, I could start a business." His disempowering vocabulary "if only" fine-tunes his brain to come up with further excuses why he can't start a business.

Instead of telling herself "if only," Kate says: "I don't have money, and this means I need to figure out how to bootstrap my business." Her brain receives high-quality instructions and she comes up with several ideas to start a business on a shoestring. Same problem, different words, different outcome.

It's not an unproven theory, discovered by some Martin Meadows guy. The concept that language has a big impact on our life is one of the staples of performance coach Tony Robbins' effective coaching process and has been proven to work with hundreds of thousands of people all over the world[3].

The basic premise of this concept is also the foundation of Nonviolent Communication, a communication process developed by Marshall Rosenberg[4], in which replacing one word with another can make the difference between an unproductive fight and successful communication.

Scientific research also suggests that words are powerful enough to induce a behavioral change. In one study, calling a carrot an "X-ray Vision Carrot" increased consumption of this vegetable by 16% among elementary school students[5]. And this effect isn't limited to gullible children alone — adults offered the choice in a cafeteria will rate the taste of "Traditional Cajun Red Beans With Rice" more favorably than the taste of "Red Beans With Rice" or compliment

"Grandma's Zucchini Cookies" more than those described simply as "Zucchini Cookies," even though they're eating the exact same dish[6].

As powerful as our brains are, words can fool them — and you can use this phenomenon to your benefit.

I hope that by now you're convinced that words matter on a deeper level than you think. Let's change your definition of failure to something more useful. *The American Heritage® Dictionary of the English Language* defines failure as: "The condition or fact of not achieving the desired end or ends.[7]"

If we play with this definition a little, we can develop a more empowering way to think about failure. This definition talks about the "desired end." If, instead of making your desired end solely about the final success, but instead define it as learning, you'll never again fail in the traditional sense. —You'll also start considering failure your friend, and not a reason to give up.

If you focus on the learning experience, you'll realize how flawed the common definitions of failure and success are. You build success through trial and error. It's the failure — and the lessons it provides — that turn you into a winner, not avoiding it. Sticking to what's known, easy and comfortable is a sure-fire way to *not* reach your goals.

When a shy man chats up a woman and she rejects him, did he fail or succeed? To an average person watching the interaction, the man has been rejected. He failed. But did he really?

If his intention is to overcome shyness — or in other words, to learn something — the outcome of his approach doesn't matter. His desired end is to learn how to become more confident. He was brave enough to step outside his comfort zone and talk. Viewed in terms of his purpose, a rejection might have been an even better outcome than getting a woman's phone number, because repeatedly getting rejected helps him get used to it.

In rock climbing — my favorite sport — you learn more on a difficult route you can't finish than on an easy route that you climb effortlessly. It helps you pinpoint weaknesses you need to address and uncovers your true character. Dealing with difficulties and the fear of a potential fall also sharpens your mental game and helps you become a better climber overall.

If your desired end is *learning*, is taking a fall a failure or success? Is it really better to climb an easy route and succeed (with no learning process) or fall off a difficult one, but learn something new and become a better climber?

In martial arts, for training purposes, losing can be more valuable than winning. When you lose against a more able partner, you discover your technical shortcomings. When you crush a weak rival, there's little to no learning. Is getting beaten a failure if you learned something new you otherwise wouldn't have learned?

As Josh Waitzkin notes in his book *The Art of Learning: An Inner Journey to Optimal Performance*, "Great ones are willing to get burned time and again as they sharpen their swords in the fire."[8]

Beating weak opponents, crushing easy problems, or doing things well within your comfort zone might make you look good in the eyes of other people, but it's challenging yourself that leads to improvement and long-lasting success.

Challenging yourself and persevering in spite of difficulties isn't easy by any means, and we'll spend more time with this topic in a later chapter. For now, make a mental note that failure and success are two sides of the same coin, and one cannot exist without the other.

EMPOWERING STORY #1: TURIA PITT

Turia Pitt was as successful as a 24-year old person could be. She didn't lack in anything: she was in a happy relationship, worked as a mining engineer for one of the world's largest metals and mining corporations, and in addition to her intelligence, she was also one of the Miss Earth Australia contestants.

In September 2011, she was invited to participate in a local ultramarathon through Western Australia's Kimberley region. Originally, she didn't plan to participate because of the expensive entry fee, but when the organizers waived it to have some locals participating in the race, she instantly agreed.

Turia had been running for 19 kilometers (12 miles) when she entered a gorge that forever changed her life. Due to an oversight on the part of the race organizers, she found herself in the middle of a bushfire, facing a wall of flames with no escape route.

She suffered burns to 65% of her body, lost fingers from her left hand and her thumb from the right hand. A surgeon later commented that she'd been "literally cooked" down to the bone.[9]

Multiple surgeries later, she still undergoes on average three surgeries a year and needs many more to remove the fire scars.

Fortunately, despite the horrific event and ongoing painful recovery, her spirit hasn't been broken. In 2014, she trekked a part of the Great Wall of China and raised close to $200,000 for an organization that provides free reconstructive surgery to poorer parts of the world. She continued her career in mining, received a Master's degree in mining engineering, studied for an MBA, and became a sought-out motivational speaker.

In 2015, she got engaged to her long-term partner, who had supported her throughout the years. In May 2016, she completed her first Ironman Australia competition, and just five months later completed the Ironman World Championship at Kailua-Kona, Hawaii.

As she said before departing for her trek on the Great Wall of China, "The fire has turned my life upside down; I don't want it to have any more impact. It was a couple of seconds. What's that compared to a lifetime?"[10]

When asked in an interview if she ever has bad days, she replied, "Of course. I go through dark times. But everyone has bad days. You can let experiences destroy you or mould you. I choose to let them mould me."[11]

Learn From the Failure or
Suffer the Consequences

American happiness researcher Shawn Achor points out in his book, *The Happiness Advantage: The Seven Principles of Positive Psychology That Fuel Success and Performance at Work*, that we become more successful when we are happier and more positive[12].

He provides an example of doctors, who, when put in a positive mood before making a diagnosis, show almost three times more intelligence and creativity than doctors who are in a neutral state. In addition to that, they make accurate diagnoses 19 percent faster.

Achor also writes that optimistic salespeople outsell the pessimistic ones by 56 percent and students primed to feel happy before taking math tests far outperform their "neutral" peers.

Exhibiting positivity is also one of the keys to handle failure in a constructive way and not allow it to destroy your prior achievements.

If you've ever cheated on a diet, you probably experienced the "Screw it! I messed up" thoughts. The slip-up might not have been a big issue in itself, but succumbing to these thoughts and consequently going on a full-blown cheat week ruined your prior progress. If instead you had reassured yourself it was just a small slip-up, that positive attitude would help you avoid further, more lasting negative consequences.

Neurologist Judy Willis notes in her article on re-wiring a burned-out brain that "The brain literally rewires to be more efficient in conducting information through the circuits that are most frequently activated. As you internalize your thwarted efforts to achieve your goals and interpret them as personal failure, your self-doubt and stress activate and strengthen your brain's involuntary, reactive neural networks. As these circuits become the automatic go-to networks, the brain is less successful in problem-solving and emotional control. When problems arise that previously would have been evaluated by the higher brain's reasoning, the dominant networks in the lower brain usurp control."[13]

In other words, dwelling on your failure reinforces it and makes you less effective at dealing with future failures. Turning the failure into a lesson (remember our definition of failure?) will help you to reinforce a positive coping mechanism.

I'd been trying to get down to a single digit body fat percentage for years. Each time I commenced a new workout and nutrition plan, I failed within several weeks or months upon realizing that not much had changed in my physique. To say it was frustrating would be an understatement.

After several failed attempts, I came up with a genius idea that maybe — just maybe — it would be a good idea to learn my lessons and try a completely different approach. I know, sometimes I'm not a particularly bright guy.

Upon investigating the reasons behind my past failures, I realized that I'd been making three cardinal mistakes: 1) I exercised at the gym despite not really enjoying it (hence my workouts weren't as effective as they could be); 2) I craved too quick results (which made my nutrition plan unsustainable); and 3) my motivation was too weak — enjoying a great physique wasn't a good enough reason to persist when I felt frustrated.

I heeded the lessons my failures taught me by replacing boring, frustrating bodybuilding exercises with fun, passion-filled rock climbing and krav maga – an Israeli self-defense system – workouts.

I refined my diet to deliver slow, but sustainable results that aren't spectacular on a week-to-week basis, but lead to extraordinary results on a month-to-month basis.

Lastly, I uncovered a stronger reason why I wanted to accomplish my goal: dropping body fat tremendously improved my climbing performance. I linked my weight loss to one of the biggest passions in my life, and suddenly everything was easier to handle.

In the end, the lessons I learned from past failures delivered a big impact on my general well-being and helped me get closer to reaching my goal.

EXERCISE #1: LEARN FROM FAILURE

The next time you fail, resist the temptation to let anger, frustration, discouragement or self-guilt make you give up. Give yourself time to process the negative emotions, and then make a list of the lessons you've learned from not reaching your desired outcome.

This will help you develop a positive mechanism for coping with failure. When you transform a failure into a list of lessons, you'll empower yourself by thinking in terms of possible ideas for improvement instead of poisoning yourself with negativity.

3 Metaphors You Can Use to Change Your Definition of Failure

You already know that words are powerful. I hope that now you will consider failure a valuable tool, and not a useless, frustrating and discouraging event.

You can further reframe how you think about failure by using metaphors. A word or a phrase that represents one thing while talking about another is a sneaky way to unconsciously change how you think about something.

Thinking of a certain problem as a *crushing burden* makes you associate it with an ordeal. You feel like you're too weak to *get it off your shoulders* and *breathe freely again*. How are you supposed to overcome it when merely thinking about it makes you physically shrink?

Replacing this metaphor with something more empowering — for example, thinking of a problem like a *barbell* that you *want* to *lift off the ground* to *build muscle and get stronger* — will shift your attitude to a more positive one.

Here are three metaphors you can use to further drive the point home that failure is necessary and useful:

1. Failure is like navigating a maze

If you imagine the process of working on your goal as navigating a maze, each failure teaches you what doesn't work. One by one, you're eliminating ineffective approaches. When you adopt this metaphor, failure won't mean the end. It will mean a new beginning.

It's close to impossible to escape a maze without getting yourself into a dead end or two. Isn't it interesting that some people will pay to enter a corn field maze and have the time of their lives trying to get out, but give up immediately when they get lost in the exact same—albeit metaphorical—maze when working on their goals?

2. Failure is like a sculpting tool

Michelangelo once said that "Every block of stone has a statue inside it and it is the task of the sculptor to discover it."[14]

When you adapt this metaphor, each failure will fuel your curiosity to discover the statue inside the stone you're carving. The process of carving this metaphorical stone doesn't merely shape the stone; it also shapes the sculptor. Each failure improves your carving skills and as you are slowly discovering the sculpture inside the stone you're carving, you are also uncovering a better sculptor in yourself.

3. Failure is a filter

One of my favorite metaphors for failure is that it's a filter. The longer something takes and the more patience it requires, the more people it filters out along the way. Difficult goals are often easier to reach because there's less competition if patience plays a big role in their accomplishment.

The fact that some things are hard filters out those who don't have enough resolve and rewards those who do; —it also blesses the latter—not only with success, but also immense personal growth and increased mental resilience.

When looking at failure from this perspective, you should be grateful that your goal is so difficult to achieve because it ensures that you need to go through a long, hard process that will make you a better person.

There are many stories of people who won the lottery only to lose it all, if not to end up worse off than they were before their "lucky" day. That's what happens when you score an easy win you didn't earn — you get the event (success), —but you don't get the process that shapes you to become a person who actually deserves it and knows how to handle it.

Compare those "lucky" winners with people who spend long years toiling away at their businesses, dealing with one failure after another, and pushing through. When they finally build a successful business and start earning a lot of money, they'll be infinitely less likely to lose it all. Precisely because it wasn't easy to achieve, now they'll be able to enjoy their success for decades to come.

Think of it as treating the symptoms vs. eliminating the root cause. An easy win — such as winning the lottery or undergoing a weight loss surgery — is treating the symptoms. You aren't changing as a person. Your habits stay the same and will drag you back to where you started. When you eliminate the root cause — a lack of positive habits, inaction, procrastination, or a lack of self-discipline — you'll be forever changed and your world will transform according to your internal changes.

Each time you get angry at how difficult accomplishing your goal is, remind yourself that it's a tool through which you'll gain the right for your success. If all were given to you when you asked, you wouldn't appreciate it and wouldn't become a person who knows how to handle such a reward. In the end, you would probably squander it. Let the filter work its magic and shape you like a blacksmith forges a sword.

WHAT IS YOUR DEFINITION OF FAILURE? QUICK RECAP

1. If you want to handle failure in a constructive way, change your definition of it. If you have a disempowering definition of failure, such as "failure is a lack of success", you'll avoid it as much as you can, and thus never achieve the ultimate objective you're after — personal growth. Words have power, and changing the definitions you use will change your behavior.

2. A more useful definition of failure is that you fail when you fail to learn something from an event. If you consistently step outside your comfort zone and try new things, you'll always learn something new — and that will empower you and help you achieve your long-term goals.

3. It's you who controls how much of an impact a failure will have on your performance and future progress. Resist the temptation to feel angry, frustrated, discouraged, or guilty when you fail. Instead, make a list of lessons you've learned from not reaching your desired outcome. If you repeatedly make a big deal of every tiny slip-up, you'll fine-tune your brain to react in this way for every future problem. It's a troubling behavior, because humans perform best in a positive state, not when dwelling on past mistakes, criticizing oneself or feeling guilty.

4. You can use metaphors to further change your beliefs about failure. Three powerful metaphors about failure you can use are: thinking of failure in terms of navigating a maze, in which each

failure helps you get closer to the end, looking at failure as a sculpting tool, and considering failure a filter that eliminates people who aren't dedicated enough.

PART 1: 7 Types of Failure and How to Handle Them

When I was 18, I came up with an idea to launch a clothing brand with my then best friend. We designed a logo, manufactured our first t-shirts, and talked about our exciting plans for the future of the brand. However, when the moment arrived to register the company and obtain funding, my soon-to-be formal business partner showed that he wasn't as serious about the idea as I had hoped. I had to pressure him into meetings with potential people who could lend us money. I quickly realized that it would be better to take my losses and terminate the idea before we launched a business that would be destined to fail — along with ending our friendship.

In hindsight, it was a surprisingly wise decision, considering I was only 18 and had little business experience. It stung to watch my dream of owning a clothing company die before it was even born, but it was a necessary milestone in my business life.

This story is but one example of failure I experienced in my life. Failure comes in many flavors, and I tasted them all. In this part, each chapter will cover a common type of failure, provide some examples and address how to handle it in the most effective way.

Please note that a failure can belong to multiple categories, so sometimes you'll need to mix two approaches to handle your specific situation. Even if you don't feel that a certain type of failure applies to you, I suggest that you read this chapter in its entirety, so you can understand how people set themselves up for a failure, process it in an unconstructive way, and/or how they can prevent it from happening again.

Chapter 2: Dealing With a Failure You Couldn't Prevent

A failure that you couldn't prevent should be the easiest failure to handle — after all, you couldn't have prevented it — but unfortunately, it's often the most challenging one to process.

One of the most common and painful examples is losing a job due to the company cutting costs. Getting fired with no prior notice, virtually overnight, can become one of the most traumatic events in life.

Another example of a negative event that you often can't prevent is a breakup of a relationship or being cheated on. The dreaded "I need to tell you something" conversation doesn't always come with a prior notification. Naturally, the longer you were in the relationship, the more difficult it is to recover. Just like an unexpected job loss, losing a key relationship in your life can result in long-term trauma.

Is there anything you can do to prepare yourself for a negative event that you can't prevent or to recover from it more quickly?

Is a failure sometimes indeed unpreventable or is there something you can always do to reduce the risk of it happening?

That's what we'll talk about in this chapter — and here's where Stoicism comes into play. This ancient Greek school of philosophy proposes several fundamental principles to live by. While they all can be useful and valuable to a modern person, the tenets we're most interested in for the purpose of this chapter are the following:

1. Accept what can't be changed

Arrian, a 2nd-century disciple of the prominent Greek Stoic Epictetus opens his *Enchiridion of Epictetus* (a Stoic manual based on the teachings of Epictetus) with the following words: "Some things are in our control and others not."[15]

Whenever you find yourself angry at a situation you can't change, remind yourself that it's not up to you. I know that it sounds oversimplistic, but as counterintuitive as it is, accepting that things are beyond your control will give you a sense of peace and enable you to move on. After all, there's nothing else you can do, so why not accept that the matter is settled and move on?

You dress according to the weather and not according to what you'd like the weather to be like. Staying angry when you can't influence a situation is not only unproductive, —it's also like giving yourself an unnecessary punishment.

Stoicism is based on the concept that peace of mind comes from focusing on what you *can* control instead of wasting your energy on things you can't change. According to the Stoics, the only things you can *always* control are your own thoughts and subsequent beliefs, attitudes, and actions. Everything else — whatever is *not* your own thought, belief or action — is outside of your total control, so getting annoyed when something doesn't go your way is a waste of resources.

This doesn't mean that Stoics exhibited learned helplessness because they couldn't fully control the world around them. Stoicism has never been about fatalism. Accepting that certain things are beyond your control doesn't mean that you should stop any efforts to improve yourself. Rather, it's about not dwelling on things not going your way, which in turn frees up mental energy to focus on the things that you *do* control.

A great habit to cultivate to become better at accepting that you can't change certain things is to deliberately introduce uncomfortable changes in your life. By stepping outside your comfort zone, you'll learn how to adapt to unfamiliar situations, and this skill will then help you react with more resilience to an unplanned negative situation over which you can't exert control. For example, I've already slept in a car on a couple of occasions. If I'm forced to live out of my car, sleeping in it won't be outside my comfort zone.

When facing a situation that you can't change, another way to process negative feelings is to acknowledge your emotions. Try to find the root reason why you're feeling them. Ask yourself what they're trying to tell you and how you can accomplish your original goal in the new situation.

Resisting your negative emotions, or worse, venting at everything and everyone is a sure-fire way to suffer more than necessary. As the old adage goes, pain is inevitable, but suffering is optional.

2. Practice misfortune

Stoics suggested practicing misfortune and visualizing negative things happening in your life. By imagining yourself in or actually putting yourself in a situation that mimics a possible negative event, you can practice your reaction to it, and that can help you build the mental resilience to handle such circumstances in the future. It gives you tremendous control over your life because whatever it throws at you, you'll already have a plan B to bounce back.

Note that while you often can't control what happens, you can *always* control your emotions. Practicing misfortune helps you get better at handling your emotional reactions.

This can be as simple as taking a cold shower or camping out in the wilderness. Going without modern luxuries is difficult at first, but you quickly get used to the new circumstances. In the future, whenever you won't have access to hot running water, a comfortable bed, or even a roof over your head, you'll quickly readapt. —After all, you've already experienced it and have probably developed alternative ways to take care of your hygiene or ensure a good night's sleep.

EXERCISE #2: IMAGINE THE WORST-CASE SCENARIO

Imagining the worst-case scenario each time you're faced with difficulties isn't exactly a pleasant strategy. However, if done occasionally, it can be a powerful exercise to gain better control over your emotions.

The goal is to visualize the worst thing happening, but instead of doing it out of fear or pessimism, you're doing it to plan for the future or as a reminder that what you have today might disappear tomorrow.

Thinking about losing your job and imagining how bad it would be allows you to prepare for the unexpected while you're still in a secure position. What *specifically* would you do if you had lost your job? How much time would you have to find a new source of income if they fired you today? What actions could you immediately take to bounce back as quickly as possible?

Again — you aren't doing it to feel pessimistic or out of an assumption that all the good things in your life will disappear overnight. You're doing it as an exercise in acceptance and as a reminder that it *might potentially* happen.

Stoics like to say that you never *lose* things — you *return* them. Stoics believe that you're only a temporary custodian of all the blessings you have in your life — including property, relationships, money, etc. You may get to be a temporary custodian for the rest of your life, or you may lose them sooner. Acceptance of either outcome will help you feel happier and make you more resilient.

In addition to coming up with constructive ways of dealing with the problem, ask yourself if your worst-case scenario is really so bad.

If you're reading this book, you're already in a privileged position. Millions of people all over the world can't afford to buy even a single book. Even if you lost your job today and you had no savings, you could always get help somewhere. You could ask your friends or family for help. You could go eat at a soup kitchen. You could take a dead-end job just to support yourself financially while looking for better opportunities.

Your worst-case scenario *would* affect your life negatively. I'm not downplaying how unpleasant it would feel, but most likely it would be a short-term situation that you could remedy relatively quickly, as long as you would care about changing it.

Again, I'm *not* downplaying how difficult life is for the homeless or the poor. Turning your life around can take years, and in some places or in some circumstances it's more challenging than in others. However, there are still plenty of examples of people rising out of poverty or homelessness. Even the worst circumstances can be temporary, as long as you maintain a tight grip on what you *can* control — your thoughts and actions.

33

3. Everything is temporary

Stoics understood that everything in life is temporary. You can be in a relationship today and be single tomorrow. You can drive an expensive car and live in a mansion today and rent a small room and use your feet as a means of transport a year from now. You can be perfectly healthy now, and bedridden next week.

My friend has a stable, enviable job in a multinational S&P 500 corporation with a long history and great prospects for the future. As the only expert in his domain in his area, his position is as secure as it could be. Yet, he still periodically browses through job offers and keeps in touch with headhunters.

You could say that since his position is so secure, there's no way he could ever lose his job. But as a shrewd person, he recognizes that everything is temporary. Even if the worst happens and he gets fired due to the factors outside his control, he'll be prepared thanks to his policy of keeping eyes open for new opportunities.

EXERCISE #3: A DISTURBING GOODBYE

A powerful, but let's admit it — disturbing — exercise you can perform to improve the key relationships in your life is to imagine it's the last time you're seeing the other person.

As morbid as it sounds, sometimes I remind myself that every important person in my life can disappear from it literally overnight. Being in the wrong place at the wrong time is all it takes to lose a life.

Would I really want our last interaction to be negative? Would I really get angry over a little, insignificant thing? Would I really want to waste time arguing instead of enjoying each other's company?

This practice will help you stop taking people for granted — and that will help your relationships flourish because whenever you'll slip back into negative communication habits, imagining it's the last time you're seeing another person will shake you back into the realization that things *are* temporary and remind you how fragile life is.

It all sounds dire and grim to think about negative events, but it doesn't mean that if you want to follow Stoicism, you need to be fatalistic or pessimistic. It's not about living your life as if it were a life sentence of suffering. Rather, it's about accepting the world how it *is*, so you can maintain good spirits even when things aren't going well. In essence, Stoicism is about maximizing your happiness, no matter what the circumstances may be.

When you land in trouble or suffer a terrible blow, espousing the belief that everything is temporary will help you handle it more quickly. —After all, as the old adage says, "This too shall pass." You might be in debt today, but if you work on eliminating it, eventually you'll be free of it. It's not a permanent condition that's beyond your control. Likewise, —a success can be also short-lived, so when you live according to this philosophy, you'll be more watchful to keep the good things in your life instead of resting on your laurels.

EXERCISE #4: WHAT DO YOU TAKE FOR GRANTED?

It's easy to believe that the things you have in your life will be there forever. This erroneous belief can make you complacent and consequently increase the risk of losing those things. Spend a few minutes making a list of things you take for granted. For example, you could write:

1. My partner.

2. My business.

3. My health.

4. Hot running water.

5. Electricity.

6. A comfortable bed to sleep on.

7. A smartphone.

Now, focus on the relationships and achievements on your list. Ask yourself if you're indeed paying enough attention to them. Taking those things for granted can make you stop putting enough effort to maintain them. This can increase the risk of losing those things, —and when it *does* happen, it produces a shock that often feels like it couldn't have been prevented. After all, you thought it was yours forever, so how in the world could you have ever predicted you would lose it?

Take action today, even if it feels like everything is perfect. Make an extraordinary effort to not merely maintain them, but also to take the relationships and achievements in your life to the next level.

Surprise your partner by planning a romantic weekend getaway to a cabin in the mountains. Resist being complacent in your business by taking a big risk to expand it to another market or by making some improvements in your daily processes. Even if you feel perfectly healthy, do bloodwork to make sure everything is fine. And even if it is, make an effort to further improve your diet and fitness levels.

DEALING WITH A FAILURE YOU COULDN'T PREVENT: QUICK RECAP

1. The first common type of failure is failure that you can't prevent. In contrast to other failures, as the name implies, you usually can't prevent it. Fortunately, there's a lot you *can* do to handle it better. The most powerful approach is adopting the philosophy of Stoicism and the stance that if something is beyond your control, you need to accept it and move on.

2. Practice acceptance by deliberately introducing uncomfortable changes, not resisting your emotions (venting or denial only makes things worse), and reminding yourself that some things are not up to you, and it should actually become a source of comfort for you because the matter is settled and you're free to move on.

3. Practicing misfortune by envisioning negative events or creating uncomfortable circumstances is a good way to increase the control you have over your own emotions because ultimately, it's one of the few things you *do* control.

4. Lastly, remember that everything is temporary. Embracing this philosophy can help you in two ways: you'll stop taking things for granted and put in more effort to maintain them, and you'll get better at handling blows. —After all, everything is temporary, and so is pain.

Chapter 3: Dealing With a Failure Due to Unrealistic Expectations

Professor and psychologist Janet Polivy posits that people don't behave logically when time and time again they try to introduce a change in their lives despite previous failures.

According to her concept of the "false hope syndrome," many individuals are stuck in a cycle in which they have unrealistic expectations about accomplishing their goals. They tend to be wrong about the speed, amount, ease, and consequences of their attempts.[16] They try, fail, brood over it, process it, and try again, but with the same unrealistic expectations, which guarantees yet another failure.

Bob wants to lose 50 pounds as quickly as possible. He sets a goal to burn excess fat within three months. This new diet he just read about looks easy, and after all, what's so difficult about losing weight?

When he steps on the scales two weeks later, he realizes he's only lost 4 pounds. There's also little difference in his appearance. Frustrated at the slow pace and his restrictive crash diet, he gorges on fast food for the entire week.

A month passes. Bob realizes he really needs to lose weight. He'll reach it this time, he assures himself. He just didn't try hard enough with his previous attempt. He picks a new popular diet — *this one will surely work* — and starts again. Three weeks later, Bob is seen filling his shopping cart with so much junk food that he can barely push the cart to the counter.

This process repeats over and over again. After each failure, Bob rejects the notion that his approach is flawed. He either didn't try hard enough or it was the wrong diet. He never questions that maybe it's not about little adjustments, but that his entire approach needs to change to one of focusing on sustainable results and permanent changes.

As Janet Polivy asks in her paper, "Do those who succeed on their sixth attempt succeed by using, once again, the same strategy that failed on the previous five attempts? Or do those who succeed on the sixth attempt do so because they have adjusted their strategy to make it more realistic and therefore more likely to succeed?"

If you repeatedly fail with the same goal, it's possible you set unrealistic expectations and are stuck in the false hope loop. Here are three principles to avoid chasing impossible goals:

1. Do proper research

Ignorance is the culprit of the false hope syndrome. A person who wants to make a positive change in their life will exhibit overexcitement and a readiness to start as quickly as possible — usually at the expense of doing proper research.

Note that this usually happens to a person who doesn't know much about the goal they want to reach. Elon Musk can say that he'll send people to Mars within a decade because he's already an extremely accomplished entrepreneur and knows a lot about the space industry. Your neighbor Joe is an unlikely space pioneer, unless he happens to be a billionaire astrophysicist. He would make a better start in the business world by building an e-commerce store or a landscaping company.

To avoid failing due to unrealistic expectations, make sure to carefully research the feasibility of your goals. Can you really lose 10 pounds a week? Does an average entrepreneur build a six-figure business in six months? Has any world-class performer become one after a mere year of training?

Explore different strategies to reach your goal, primarily focusing on the ones that have been proven to work for numerous people before. A revolutionary system to become a golf star within six weeks might sound exciting, but it's the plain old regular practice — day in, day out for years — that delivers real-world, sustainable results.

(Side note: I cover in great detail how to do proper research and choose a winning strategy in my book *The Ultimate Focus Strategy: How to Set the Right Goals, Develop Powerful Focus, Stick to the Process, and Achieve Success.*)

2. Be open to changing your approach

If you've already failed a couple of times and want to try again, consider completely changing your approach, rather than trying the same approach again and expecting different results. Perhaps the approach you've taken isn't founded on healthy principles or doesn't work in your unique situation.

When you close your mind to alternative approaches, you can get stuck in the failure loop forever. It's like trying to dig a metro tunnel with a trowel. No matter how hard you work, you won't accomplish it in your lifetime. What you need is professional machinery, not more energy to dig with a trowel.

I used to follow the traditional bodybuilding method of bulking up to gain muscle and then going on a diet to shed excess body fat. I was so set on this strategy that I wouldn't even consider that there was another way to improve my physique — even when the approach clearly didn't work for me, no matter how strict I was about it. Fortunately, multiple failures later I finally saw the light and decided to completely change my approach.

I spent over five years launching one business after another. The process was virtually the same every time — a new idea, a lot of enthusiasm, first steps, first problems, failure, depression, another new idea, another failure, rinse and repeat. Instead of picking one solid business idea and sticking to it no matter what, I gave myself failure after failure. Once again, —if I hadn't opened my mind to a new approach, I wouldn't have reached my goal.

If you've had similar experiences, drop all of your preconceived notions and try again with a completely different approach. Don't be afraid to experiment with a strategy that is opposite to what you've been sticking to until now. Being flexible is one of the most powerful traits for success.

3. Accept that things rarely go as planned

Peter Drucker once said that most people overestimate what they can do in one year and underestimate what they can do in ten years.

Before the construction of the countryside house for my parents commenced (I've previously mentioned that financing this project was one of my most important reasons to build a successful business), everyone told me that in construction, everything takes twice as long and costs twice as much. I didn't believe it. After all, if you hire the right team and budget properly, it's impossible that such a thing can happen, right?

How wrong I was. Everything *did* cost much more and *did* take much longer. It made me realize that even with the most careful calculations, you'll probably still overestimate how much you can achieve in a given period of time. If you refuse to accept this reality, say hello to the failure loop.

When setting a new goal and deadline, remind yourself that ultimately even if you don't achieve something by your self-imposed deadline, you're still farther ahead. It's illogical to quit because during 3 months you've lost *just* 10 pounds instead of 20. Yet, that's precisely what many people do. They assume that since things didn't go *exactly* as planned, they failed. Then they get frustrated, turn to junk food to reassure themselves, and a few weeks later, the 10 pounds they've lost are back.

To sum up, to avoid failure due to unrealistic expectations, focus on two key actions:

1. Ensure that your expectations are realistic by performing thorough research. Putting on rose-colored glasses and living in the world of happy ignorance is *not* a good way to reach your goals. There'll be time for moonshot goals once you become an expert and can accurately estimate the probability of reaching those big dreams.

2. Develop patience and accept that even if you're the greatest project manager in the world, you'll still fail to account for every surprise, delay, and setback. What's important isn't reaching the goal by a given deadline — it's reaching the goal, period.

EMPOWERING STORY #2: PETER DIAMANDIS

Upon discovering that Charles Lindbergh flew from New York to Paris in 1927 to win a $25,000 prize, engineer, physician, and entrepreneur Peter Diamandis came up with an idea to offer an incentive prize to build and fly a reusable private spaceship.

In May 1996, without the prize money in hand, Peter went onstage under the St. Louis Gateway Arch and announced the $10 million XPRIZE to build and fly a reusable private spaceship carrying three people into space on two flights within two weeks.

He thought that he would easily find a sponsor. Moreover, the prize was to be paid after the spaceship successfully completed both flights, and you don't exactly build a spaceship in a few weeks so there was plenty of time to find the right benefactor.

Except it didn't work out as Peter expected. Between 1996 and 2001 he would pitch to over 150 sponsors — and get rejected 150 times.

Fortunately, his persistence and grit eventually paid off when in 2002 — six years after announcing the prize — he met the Ansari family who ultimately funded the $10 million prize. The prize was paid out on October 4, 2004 to the SpaceShipOne team led by American designer Burt Rutan.

Today, the XPRIZE Foundation has awarded over $300 million in XPRIZEs designed to encourage technological development and radical breakthroughs for the benefit of humanity.

As Peter said in his article about his breakthroughs, "If I had to name my superpower, it would be persistence (or grit) — i.e. not giving up, even when everyone is telling me that it isn't going to work."[17]

DEALING WITH A FAILURE DUE TO UNREALISTIC EXPECTATIONS: QUICK RECAP

1. The second common type of failure is failure due to unrealistic expectations. Some people get stuck in a cycle in which they set unreasonable expectations, fail, try again, and fail again due to being unrealistic with what they can accomplish.

2. To prevent this failure from happening, make sure to do proper research before setting a goal. Ignorance leads to unrealistic expectations, which leads to failure. Be particularly careful when you're a newbie. Assume you'll achieve average results and focus on proven strategies instead of seeking magic pills.

3. Be open to changing your approach if your current strategy isn't working. Being stubborn when your approach isn't effective won't magically make it work.

4. Accept that things rarely go as planned. It might take you longer to reach your goal than you'd like, and you'll probably overestimate what you can achieve in a short period of time. Be patient.

Chapter 4: Dealing With a Failure Due to a Lack of Focus

In today's world of never-ending busyness and hundreds of tasks to do, failure due to a lack of focus is one of the most common reasons why people can't achieve their goals. In fact, I believe this problem is the biggest hurdle for accomplishment, and that's why I wrote an entire book about it, *The Ultimate Focus Strategy: How to Set the Right Goals, Develop Powerful Focus, Stick to the Process, and Achieve Success*.

The fundamental rule of the Ultimate Focus Strategy is that the more goals you have, the less likely you are to achieve them. I strongly recommend limiting your objectives to no more than three, and ideally just one or two, that you'll be working on every day, or as often as you can. Working on numerous goals in different walks of life at once means inevitably neglecting some of them.

At one point, I practiced five different sports — bodybuilding, rock climbing, krav maga, tennis, and swimming. I also took frequent walks and went on bike rides. Needless to say, I couldn't really focus properly on any of those activities and progress quickly.

I had to quit bodybuilding, tennis, and swimming — sports that I had been failing at anyway and didn't enjoy as much — so I could improve quickly in rock climbing and krav maga — sports that I find more entertaining and challenging. If it hadn't been for quitting those sports, I know I would have continued to fail. My performance would have been heavily affected by a lack of focus.

In my book, I cover in great detail how to focus on the right goals in the long term, but for a quick summary, here are the basic guidelines that will help you eliminate the risk of failing due to spreading yourself too thin:

1. Sacrifice is necessary. Sacrificing less-important goals will give you more power to work on the most crucial objectives. Prioritize big life improvements like changing your diet, getting a better job, starting a business, or finding a life partner, over less significant objectives.

2. Embrace boredom. It's exciting to set new goals or follow new strategies, but if you prioritize excitement over effectiveness, you'll only lose focus and possibly fail. If something works, stick to it.

3. Pare it down. Each time you're struggling with prioritizing your tasks, consider which task can make other tasks irrelevant or easier, and do that one first. Resist the temptation to procrastinate by first doing the easiest tasks on your to-do list. Instead, find a way to perform a task that will permanently take those less important tasks off your list.

One of the world's most successful venture capitalists, Chris Sacca, founder of Lowercase Capital and a guest shark on ABC's reality television show Shark Tank, wrote in his blog post announcing his goodbye to the venture capital world the following paragraph:

"The only way I know to be awesome at startups is to be obsessively focused and pegged to the floor of the deep-end, gasping for air. I succeeded at venture capital because, for years, I rarely thought about or spent time on anything else. Anything less than that unmitigated full commitment leaves me feeling frustrated and ineffective. As you've heard me say on the show, if I'm not all-in, I'm out."[18]

If you're working on a particularly challenging goal, the "all-in or out" approach might be the only way forward, and it certainly won't hurt if you decide to follow this philosophy at least partly and greatly limit your focus.

EXERCISE #5: FOCUS TO THE EXTREME

It's incredible how much you can achieve if you focus on one key goal and disregard everything else. While most people will find it impossible to have a single focus in life — there are always many obligations to attend to — try to set aside a weekend or perhaps even an entire week, during which you'll only work on one key goal.

Successful entrepreneur Craig Ballantyne suggests in his article, "You Have Never Thought This Way Before" that if you want to finish your product and start a business, "Book a hotel conference room if you must. Pay the money upfront so you won't back out. Arrive there early and lock yourself in and don't come out until you have a product to
put online."[19]

You can use this strategy to finish a long overdue project, write your first short book, publish an important blog post or article, memorize key words and phrases in a foreign language, or complete virtually every other goal you can work on in a hotel room.

If you're working on other goals like lowering your highly-elevated cholesterol levels, spend the entire weekend or week paying extremely close attention to your diet by noting down every single piece of food you put in your mouth. Read a couple of books about the dangers of elevated cholesterol levels. Religiously stick to the recommended workout schedule.

The point is to become as immersed in your goal as possible. Even if you can't maintain a given routine in the long term, you'll still benefit from this short-term exercise to remind you of the power that lies inside you if you double down on what's most important to you.

DEALING WITH A FAILURE DUE TO A LACK OF FOCUS: QUICK RECAP

1. The third common type of failure is caused by a lack of focus. Whenever you spread your attention over too many different goals, you'll hinder your performance. This will likely lead to rapid failure because it's impossible to reach key goals without sacrificing less significant objectives.

2. To avoid this type of failure, make sure to prioritize big goals and dedicate most of your energy to them. Realize that you can't have your cake and eat it, too. Limiting your focus is necessary for success.

3. Embrace boredom and stick to the things that are working well for you, even if they're no longer as exciting as they were in the beginning.

4. Lastly, focus on the essence of the goal you want to reach. Oftentimes you can pinpoint just one key action that will make every other action easier or unnecessary. Do this action to gain more clarity and focus.

Chapter 5: Dealing With a Fear-Driven Failure

Failure driven by fear is one of the most common reasons why people fail to act on their goals or give up prematurely. There are a few different causes of fear, so let's discuss them one by one:

1. Fear of the unknown

As strange as it sounds, people unconsciously often *want* to fail. They subconsciously live by the motto that a known devil is better than an unknown angel. It's easier to let the things stay as they are — even if you're not entirely happy with them — than to be bold and venture out, seeking greener pastures.

A good example of failing due to the fear of the unknown is sticking to your current day job even when you absolutely hate it. Obviously, it isn't sensible to quit without a solid plan — the failure lies in the fact that even though you hate your job, you do nothing to change it because you're afraid of the unknown.

If you set for yourself a life-changing goal, this means that you need to leave your safe bubble and travel to unknown, potentially dangerous places. It's scary, so it's no wonder that many people sabotage their efforts to avoid this fear.

The only solution to overcome this behavior is to slowly, but consistently, stretch your comfort zone and resist the temptation to default to security. While the need for safety is a basic human need we all share, too much of it doesn't go hand in hand with growth. If you want to take your life to the next level, you'll have to sacrifice some of that security for growth.

The first time I climbed a 100-feet-high cliff (30 meters), I was extremely scared. When I stood exposed on the rock face, with the wind blowing at me strongly and surrounded by open space in all directions, I felt the temptation to ask my belayer to lower me. It would be nice to touch the ground again and feel safe, but I wouldn't have learned anything that way. I pushed ahead, overcame my fear and completed the route.

After so many scary experiences, I still feel queasy or even get panicky at times. If you keep challenging yourself, those feelings will never leave you. You just learn to push through them more effectively.

And don't misunderstand me — there's nothing glorious in being frightened. When I'm scared, I'm *scared*. I wonder why I'm yet again doing such a thing to myself. You'll absolutely *hate* the feeling when experiencing it, but you'll look at it with great fondness and gratitude later on when you realize how much it has helped you grow.

Remember than in the end the only way to deal with the fear of the unknown is to embrace the situation as a learning opportunity — even if it's initially disconcerting.

2. Fear of rejection

Another type of fear-driven failure that keeps you stuck in the same circumstances — even if you'd love to change them — is failure due to the fear of rejection.

A common manifestation of this type of failure is not approaching a person you find attractive simply because you're afraid they'll reject you. Working in sales also requires you to overcome the fear of rejection. If you don't overcome it, you'll have lackluster, if any, results.

From a logical standpoint, as uncomfortable as a rejection can be, choosing to *not* approach an attractive person or try to make a sale is a guaranteed failure. If you don't ask, the answer is always no.

Unfortunately, in a situation where you face a possible rejection, following the logical thought process is challenging. I know what I'm talking about: —to battle my extreme shyness, I approached fifty attractive women in the street over a span of three months. I wasn't looking for any specific outcome other than to overcome my paralyzing fear and approach them. I didn't want to create an awkward situation or get rejected, so at first I found it extremely difficult to act.

In the end, my fears were unfounded. Most women didn't mind that I approached them; in fact, many were eager to talk with me, and I discovered that being rejected by a great majority of them wasn't such a big deal. In the end, exposing myself to repeated rejections eradicated shyness from my life.

Learning how to deal with rejection can change your life, too. Just like with the fear of the unknown, you immunize yourself against rejection through consistent desensitization.

Forget about the end goal you're trying to achieve (making a sale, setting up a date) and aim for rejection. If your ultimate goal is to get rejected, then if you get rejected, you aren't losing anything. After all, that's what you were seeking. If you don't get rejected, though — good for you. You acted despite your fear and programmed your mind that facing fears head on is worth it.

A crucial aspect in overcoming the fear of rejection is to not let the emotions cloud your judgment. Whenever you're in a situation that causes you to withdraw because of a possible rejection, don't give yourself even a second to think about it. For instance, if you see an attractive person standing by themselves in a shopping mall and you'd like to talk with them, go and talk to them right away. The longer you hesitate, the less likely you'll be to act.

Bestselling author Tim Ferriss writes in his book *The 4-Hour Workweek* that "A person's success in life can usually be measured by the number of uncomfortable conversations he or she is willing to have."[20] My personal experience confirms that dealing with the fear of rejection isn't optional; —it's crucial to achieve most goals.

3. Fear of losing your identity

In addition to being afraid of a possible change, people fail because their identity is wrapped around certain negative aspects of their lives.

Often, an obese person — even when they know that obesity is bad for them — feels good with being obese because eating a lot is who they think they are. They define themselves as being "big-boned" and as being "wired" to gorge on fast food.

Granted, not everyone has this problem, and I'm not singling out people with weight problems. I was overweight in my late teens, and I drew certain pleasure out of being called "Big Martin," so I know how it feels. Likewise, in some twisted way, I enjoyed being an entrepreneur who constantly failed. I felt proud that I kept trying, — even though it would have served me more to stop being proud of my struggles and probe into why I'd been failing so much.

Again, it's definitely not comfortable to realize that you actually *like* struggling, but it might be the biggest stumbling block that separates you from success.

It's important to acknowledge that the biggest failure in life is to remain the same person throughout the years. As they say, if you're not growing, you're dying. Merely acknowledging that you have a fondness for certain negative aspects of your life can help you take the first step to defeat it.

Last but not least, don't romanticize the fact that you're struggling. Pride yourself on overcoming your circumstances instead of drawing significance out of your hardships.

In her speech at the Harvard University, J. K. Rowling, author of *Harry Potter*, the best-selling book series in history, said "Poverty entails fear, and stress, and sometimes depression; it means a thousand petty humiliations and hardships. Climbing out of poverty by your own efforts, that is indeed something on which to pride yourself, but poverty itself is romanticised only by fools."[21]

I used to be extremely insecure as a teenager. I couldn't talk to women and I couldn't fit into a group. I considered myself ugly because I suffered from a bad case of acne. As twisted as it sounds, I must have at least partly enjoyed and glorified being this awkward, bizarre shy guy. Oh, what a special snowflake I was. I'm forever grateful that one day I opened my eyes and doubled down on climbing out of that perception. As Rowling said, *that's* something I can pride myself on — not the fact that I was insecure.

EMPOWERING STORY #3: SIDNEY POITIER

Accomplished Bahamian-American actor and cultural symbol Sidney Poitier recounts in his book *Life Beyond Measure* that the first, most significant turning point in his career was when he picked up a local newspaper and browsed through the job listings looking for a job as a dishwasher. Not seeing anything of interest, he turned to toss the paper into the trash when his eyes caught the theatrical listings and an ad saying in bold type "Actors Wanted."

With his curiosity piqued, he read the article below the headline and discovered that the production was to be cast at a place called the American Negro Theatre in Harlem. Realizing the theater wasn't far away from where he was standing, he decided to attend the audition.

With only a few years of formal schooling, he struggled to read aloud from a book to the director who was conducting the audition. His heavy Bahamian accent wasn't exactly helpful, either.

The director snatched the book out of his hand, spun him around and marched him to the door. He bellowed: "Get out of here and stop wasting people's time. Why don't you go out and get yourself a job as a dishwasher or something? You can't read, you can't talk, you're no actor!" Then he threw Sidney out and slammed the door shut.

As Poitier was walking back to the bus stop to continue his search for a dishwashing job, a thought occurred to him.

As he recalls: "Why did he recommend my going out and getting a job as a dishwasher? Not once during the audition did I tell him that I was a dishwasher, so why did he say it? And what became clear to me was that dishwashing was his view of my value as a human being. In that moment, I made the choice that I could not and would not allow that to stand. Now, what was I operating on? I was operating on what I learned from my mom, and what I learned from my dad—that I am somebody. I was always somebody. And here this guy who didn't know me from Adam had fashioned for me a life that I could not allow to happen if I had anything to do with it. I decided then and there, in that pivotal moment, to be an actor, if only to show this man and myself that I could.[22]"

Soon after the audition, after completing a shift at a dishwashing job, Sidney was browsing through the newspaper when an older waiter asked him what was new in the paper. Embarrassed, Sidney admitted that he couldn't read well. The waiter offered to teach him, and on many nights that followed, Sidney learned how to read. He also got rid of his Bahamian accent.

On his second attempt at the theater, he was given a leading role in the Broadway production *Lysistrata*. More roles soon followed. In 1963, as the first actor of African descent to do so, he won the Academy Award for Best Actor for his role in *Lilies of the Field*.

In 1980, he directed comedy *Stir Crazy*, which for many years was the highest-grossing film directed by a person of African descent. In 2002, in recognition of his "remarkable accomplishments as an artist and as a human being," he received an Academy Honorary Award from the Academy of Motion Picture Arts and Sciences. In 2009, he was awarded the Presidential Medal of Freedom by President Barack Obama.

And to realize it all started with one rude director and Sidney's resolution not to let him belittle his value as a human being…

4. Fear of losing connection

People get a sense of connection when they feel bad. Having problems gives you a sliver of empathy from other people that feels better than going out there, facing risks, and ultimately building a life others envy.

As sad as it sounds, most people will be friendlier and more empathetic to poor Jim who can barely cover the rent than to Stephanie, a highly accomplished self-made businesswoman who makes them feel insignificant because of her feats. Victimhood isn't a good way to become an accomplished person, but it does provide some level of comfort and security that makes certain people remain in their safe bubble.

When you reach success, you'll face envy from critics. Some people will start questioning your intentions. You'll outgrow certain people and possibly make new enemies.

Accept that reaching your goals inevitably means dealing with some of those problems. However, it doesn't mean that if you reach success, you'll never get support again. Actually, the first step to deal with the fear of losing connection is to ensure that the support system you have in place will be there for you when you grow tired of making yourself a victim. A lasting support system is usually made up of two groups of people:

- Your closest friends and family, who've been there with you no matter what. It's one of the most valuable things you can have in life. If you have those individuals, you won't need much else social-wise to succeed. They will be there to encourage you throughout the entire journey — and you should be there to encourage them throughout their own journeys.

- People who have already achieved success or are striving to reach it like you do. It's not a big deal if you don't know such people yet. When you start working on your goals, you'll naturally build this support group.

If you want to become a professional artist, surrounding yourself with fellow artists — ideally those who are more successful than you are — will give you a stronger sense of connection than trying to explain to your non-artist friends *why on Earth you want to paint those useless paintings* or record these *stupid* songs.

If you want to become a rock climber, fellow climbers will be more than eager to infect you with their passion and help you develop your skills.

If you want to get your financial life in order, personal finance bloggers and the members of personal finance forums will support your hard decisions and offer you a sense of belonging.

In the same speech I already cited, J. K. Rowling said: "I was convinced that the only thing I wanted to do, ever, was to write novels. However, my parents, both of whom came from impoverished backgrounds and neither of whom had been to college, took the view that my overactive imagination was an amusing personal quirk that would never pay a mortgage, or secure a pension."

Imagine that. If the parents of a woman who eventually became an extremely successful novelist couldn't offer her support and considered her goal an amusing quirk, then you certainly shouldn't feel bad if you're in the same position.

If you want to quit your cushy corporate job, but everyone around you is stuck in the rat race and can't imagine another way of living, don't expect them to support you in your goal as well as people who are on track to quit or have already done so would.

It's key to understand that, try as you might, you're not going to change other people's deeply-held beliefs about certain important issues. I couldn't persuade my parents that one could succeed in life without going to college. They only believed me when I started making more money than 99.9% of people of my age.

For several years I was building my business with little to no understanding and support from other people. I didn't have much encouragement and I had to believe in myself. Following the writings of successful entrepreneurs and exchanging messages with them has helped me stick to my resolutions until I finally had a breakthrough. If you can't find support elsewhere, turn to books and the Internet and I'm sure you'll find reassurance there.

In conclusion, if you're failing because you feel like it's you against the world, try to build a social bubble that will support your endeavors — even if it merely consists of online strangers on a discussion forum or a stack of books written by people you admire.

DEALING WITH A FEAR-DRIVEN FAILURE: QUICK RECAP

1. The fourth type of failure is fear-driven failure. It can be further broken down into: fear of the unknown, fear of rejection, fear of losing your identity, and fear of losing connection.

2. When dealing with a fear of the unknown and a fear of rejection, the only way to prevent that is to expose yourself to difficult and uncomfortable situations in which you face the unknown or a possible rejection. The more often you do it, the more comfortable you'll get with it. Soon you'll learn how to act despite those unpleasant emotions of discomfort, and fear will cease to be a paralyzing factor in your life.

3. When you fail because of the fear of losing your identity, it's because there are certain negative aspects of your life that you consider "you."

If you consider obesity, poverty, shyness, or any other negative trait to be a part of your identity, it's scary and uncomfortable to throw them out. However, in the end you have to stop romanticizing the bad aspects of your life and realize that life is growth. The sooner you get rid of those bad things, the better your life will become.

4. Lastly, people fear they'll lose connection when they start working on or reach their bold goals. This fear is not unfounded. Some people *will* consider your efforts a threat to their self-esteem. The best solution is to surround yourself with individuals who don't exhibit such a behavior and will actively help you reach your goals.

Chapter 6: Dealing With a Failure Due to Self-Sabotage

You can set yourself up for a failure due to low self-esteem. It can result in self-sabotaging behaviors, such as:

- not trying hard enough (after all, you don't believe you'll succeed, so what's the point of doing your best?),

- exhibiting doubt (who's going to date you, invest in your business, or hire you, if you send unconscious signals of uncertainty?),

- giving up at the first sign of trouble (why fight, if you already decided that you'd most likely fail?),

- creating situations or excuses that set a person up for a failure (like a student who parties the night before an important exam).

It's common for a person suffering from a lack of confidence to invent insignificant problems so they can have an excuse not to face the big ones.

For example, they'll tell themselves they desperately need a new dress for a job interview and spend four hours shopping instead of preparing themselves for the interview. Or they'll come up with a supposedly important reason to stay up late, so when they don't get the job they'll be able to protect their ago and say that they failed because they had to stay up late.

As absurd as it sounds, it isn't a rare behavior. Unfortunately, because it's so subtle, people usually don't notice they're doing it subconsciously — it's not like they *consciously* want to fail a job interview, but that's the outcome that their unconscious behavior produces

To overcome this type of failure, you need to take three steps:

1. Believe in your goal

A lack of confidence leads to a self-fulfilling prophecy: you don't believe you can achieve something, and that's exactly what happens. One of the most effective ways to overcome this problem is to not develop a belief in *yourself*, but in *your goal*. When you're working on an extremely important goal, increased self-confidence will be a side effect of your efforts.

I spent several years trying to build a successful business. If it weren't for my clear, deep conviction that I would literally *die* if I were to work for "the man," I wouldn't have stuck with the process for so long. I felt so strongly about the significance of this goal in my life that, even after numerous failures, getting into debt and being just an inch from having to close up shop, I didn't lose my confidence. This is what believing in the importance of your goal can do for you. Can you imagine willingly suffering so much for a goal you *sort of* want to reach?

EMPOWERING STORY #4: PHIL KNIGHT

Nike founder Phil Knight wrote the following words in his memoir, *Shoe Dog: A Memoir by the Creator of Nike*: "Driving back to Portland, I'd puzzle over my sudden success at selling. I'd been unable to sell encyclopedias, and I'd despised it to boot. I'd been slightly better at selling mutual funds, but I'd felt dead inside. So why was selling shoes so different? Because, I realized, it wasn't selling. I believed in running. I believed that if people got out and ran a few miles every day, the world would be a better place, and I believed these shoes were better to run in. People, sensing my belief, wanted some of that belief for themselves. Belief, I decided. Belief is irresistible."[23]

From then on, his life didn't magically change. While he did finally begin his work on what was to become Nike, he still went through numerous failures, setbacks, and had to deal with larger-than-life problems. However, if it wasn't for his irresistible belief, who knows if Phil would have built one of the world's largest and most recognized sports companies?

2. Replace self-handicapping with defensive pessimism or strategic optimism

When you're afraid of failure, you might sabotage your efforts to protect your ego from the crushing consequences of failure. This behavior, exhibited by creating obstacles and excuses to justify your failures, is called *self-handicapping*.

According to researchers Andrew J. Elliot and Marcy A. Church, self-handicapping makes it challenging to reach one's goals[24].

The problem with self-handicapping is that, on the surface, you always have a perfect explanation for your actions. Even if you're hurting yourself by taking actions that undermine your efforts but protect your ego, you'll still believe you're doing the right thing.

If you recognize this happening in your life, try two alternative strategies:

1. Defensive pessimism

Defensive pessimists set low expectations for their performance and envision possible negative outcomes. However, instead of creating circumstances that would undermine their success, they plan and prepare for the obstacles.[25]

This strategy focuses on managing anxiety in a constructive way. Instead of sabotaging your efforts so that you can avoid the unpleasant failure, you plan for the anxiety and develop solutions to handle it.

Let's imagine you have scheduled a job interview at your dream company. A person with a self-handicapping strategy will most likely do some of the following:

- worry themselves sick about the interview and their performance;

- unconsciously create a situation that will make them arrive late — and dramatically reduce their chance of getting hired, if they even get a second chance after being late;

- develop physical symptoms that prevent them from going to the interview, so they can avoid the anxiety (along with losing the job opportunity).

In contrast, a defensive pessimist will:

- envision a bad performance — and then research every single possible question they might be asked and prepare a solid answer for each one;

- leave to go to the interview an hour sooner, so even if there's a gigantic traffic, jam they'll still get there on time;

- ensure that they feel well and look good by paying close attention to healthy nutrition, exercise, and getting sufficient sleep prior to the job interview.

EXERCISE #6: PRACTICE DEFENSIVE PESSIMISM

If you can't exhibit optimism and often sabotage your efforts, try defensive pessimism by imagining the worst and preparing for it. The next time you find yourself preparing for a situation that produces anxiety, come up with a list of everything that can go wrong. If it's a job interview, you could jot down:

- getting sick;

- being late;

- forgetting important details about the company;

- forgetting the fundamental things you should know when applying for a given position;

- wardrobe malfunction.

Then, address every item one by one by coming up with a list of possible solutions and implement them to reduce the risk of the setback happening. Here's an example:

- Getting sick. If possible, avoid crowded places with a higher risk of an infection prior to the job interview. Eat foods and engage in habits that boost the immune system, such as exercise. Get sufficient sleep.

- Being late. Leave much sooner than necessary. Ensure that your car doesn't need any important repairs and won't suddenly break down. Charge up your phone so you can call a cab if you can't turn the engine on.

- Forgetting important details about the company. Visit the company's website and memorize everything you find interesting or good to know. Read the most recent news. Find a current employee and invite them for coffee to get insider knowledge.

- Forgetting the fundamental things you should know when applying for a given position. Review the basics of your profession. Read a book or two about the most important concepts pertaining to your job.

- Wardrobe malfunction. Prepare your clothes the evening before the job interview. Bring a second shirt or even an entire second set of clothes with you.

Assuming that everything will go wrong and then making sure that you have a contingency plan will help you overcome anxiety, build confidence and avoid self-sabotage.

2. Strategic optimism

Strategic optimists deal with the anxiety of failure by adopting the outlook that things will end well. Instead of worrying themselves sick about their future performance and trying to plan for every single possible setback, they set high expectations, visualize success, and feel calm and in control.

It takes a lot of practice to adapt this strategy if you've been a pessimist for a long time, so start small and stay patient. The process comes down to three steps:

1. Shifting your *locus of control* — the extent to which you believe you can control events that affect you[26] — from external to internal. In other words, take responsibility for your life instead of blaming everybody but you for the failure, and admit that you've achieved success thanks to your efforts, not through luck. We'll talk about locus of control in more detail later in this book.

2. Slowly stretching your comfort zone. Start with easy tasks within your comfort zone and take it from there. A string of wins — even if they're tiny — will help you build positive momentum and develop the belief that things generally turn out okay.

3. Reframing. Optimists are masterful at changing the meaning of their failures. Consequently, they don't take them personally and maintain high confidence in themselves. For example, if they don't perform well during a job interview, they'll consider it a lesson that they need to better prepare for their next interview or they'll simply tell themselves that if they didn't perform well, it was probably because subconsciously they knew it wasn't the right company for them.

(I dig deeply into the topic of self-efficacy (the strength of the belief in your abilities that can help you become more optimistic) in my free book *Confidence: How to Overcome Your Limiting Beliefs and Achieve Your Goals*.)

3. Live in a fantasy world

This will sound like a contradiction to what I've said before about being realistic, but there's a slight difference, so please read carefully…

I've been criticized that I live in a fantasy world on more than a couple of occasions. And I like when people say that because it shows how far I've gone to change my attitude (which previously was as pessimistic and self-limiting as you can get).

As much as I value being reasonable when setting new goals, I don't set limits for myself as to what I can achieve given enough time — and neither should you. This is a crucial tool to escape self-imposed mediocrity that is caused by the erroneous belief that you aren't the master of your own destiny.

This is not about believing that you can become a millionaire in three months. It's about believing that if you want it to happen, you *will* make it happen, although in a more realistic time frame. In other words, you believe that everything is possible, but you don't keep your head in the clouds.

I have a corkboard in my home office with some of my favorite quotes, and right in the center of it there are two quotes:

1. "Nothing is impossible for a man who refuses to listen to reason," from Gary Halbert, a legendary flamboyant copywriter who is responsible for some of the most successful direct mail campaigns.

If you're reading this book, I assume you're doing so because you want to build a better life for yourself. This in itself runs contrary to the behavior of a large group of people who couldn't care less about self-improvement.

Understand that you'll meet with adversity and disbelief because it clashes with how those people see the world. *You'll* be the unreasonable one in *their* eyes, but don't let it define your self-confidence. All successful people have to deal with this.

2. "To live an extraordinary life, you must resist an ordinary approach," from Frank McKinney, a self-proclaimed real estate artist, international bestselling author, philanthropist and ultramarathoner,

who has built oceanfront spec homes (homes built without an identified buyer) valued in the tens of millions of dollars.

I often re-read these quotes to imprint them even deeper in my mind, but what's more important is actually taking action in line with what they espouse. Namely, it's refusing to accept the self-limiting beliefs imposed on you by society. It's about *not* following the herd right over the cliff. It's about developing trust in yourself, because you're the expert of your own life and what you want it to be like. You won't always be right, but what's important is that you did what *you* thought was right. I'd much rather fail because *I* made the wrong choice than because I listened to someone else.

In more practical terms, this means things like:

- Quitting a lucrative job that you hate, to do something that actually gives you joy and doesn't convert your life into a nightmare. "Reasonable" people would probably say you should stick to a lucrative job. It's such a bad job market, you should be happy with what you have. But in the end, is life really about money alone, or hey, maybe — *juuuust maybe* — the point is to be happy and fulfilled?

- Going against the tide when you believe it makes sense. Most self-published authors undervalue their work by selling their books for $2.99. Readers often buy such books on impulse, skim through them and forget about them right away. I first broke the mold by pricing my books at $3.99 and $4.99, and then going as high as $7.99. It's only a few bucks more, but paying two or three times more for a book suddenly makes a reader respect their purchase more.

- Standing out, even at the risk of ridicule. Obviously, it's not about putting on underwear over your pants just to be different. A great example here is Dollar Shave Club founder Michael Dubin, who created a slapstick YouTube video promoting his new company. Instead of taking the common and boring "professional" angle for his commercial, he chose humor and sarcasm. Within just four years, it paid off handsomely when he sold the company to Unilever for $1 billion in cash.

Adopting these two outlooks on life will help you develop more trust in yourself and, consequently, overcome (or at least reduce) the occurrence of self-sabotaging behaviors.

DEALING WITH A FAILURE DUE TO SELF-SABOTAGE: QUICK RECAP

1. The fifth type of failure is failure caused by self-sabotage. When a person lacks the confidence to face their fears head on, doesn't believe that they can achieve a given goal, or (even worse) doesn't believe in their worth as a human being, they'll inevitably sabotage their efforts. This behavior usually manifests by creating excuses or situations that lead to failure or inaction.

For instance, a person will unconsciously choose to stay up late for some supposedly important reason so they can look tired during the job interview and reduce their chances of success. Then, if they fail, they'll be able to protect their ego by saying something along the lines of, "I didn't get this job because I had to stay up late."

2. The first step to deal with this type of failure is to believe in your goal. If you can't develop the confidence in yourself, develop the belief that the goal you're pursuing is something you absolutely must reach. This, as if by association, will help you develop more conviction in your abilities to make it come to pass.

3. The second step is to replace the strategy of self-handicapping (creating obstacles and excuses to avoid anxiety or justify your failures) with something more effective: defensive pessimism or strategic optimism.

Defensive pessimists envision negative outcomes and prepare themselves for every possible setback. Consequently, they have less anxiety and perform better. To become a defensive pessimist, go through your worries one by one and develop strategies to handle them.

Strategic optimists, on the other hand, assume that things will turn out okay, and that helps them manage their anxiety and perform on a high level. To become more optimistic, shift your locus of control by claiming personal responsibility for every failure and success in your life, stretch your comfort zone to gain confidence and momentum, and reframe negative events to turn them into lessons instead of excuses as to why you're a failure.

4. Lastly, live in a fantasy world. This means adopting the belief that there are no limits. While you need to be realistic about the timeframe needed to reach success, resist the social programming that tells you to remain average and conform. Dare to go against the tide whenever you feel deep inside your heart that you're right.

Chapter 7: Dealing With a Failure Due to Impatience

Impatience can make you fail in two ways: you can establish an unsustainable tempo and fail because you can't support it, or give up because your progress rate is too slow and you don't want to wait any longer. Let's address the latter problem first and then come back to the former.

1. Failure because of slow progress

We've already covered that what matters is accomplishing your goal — period — and not how long it took you to reach it.

Of course, it's frustrating when things take longer than you expected, but if you give up because your progress is too slow, then you won't make your dream come true at all. Does it really matter that it will take you longer?

Don't obsess over deadlines. Rough estimates can be helpful, but they can't dictate your life.

When I was 18, I set a goal to achieve financial independence within 7 years. In the end, it took me 9 years. Did I fail? Should I have given up after 7 years because (back then) nothing indicated that I'd reach my goal just two years later?

What's better: achieving your goal two years later than previously planned or not achieving it at all?

I used to follow this illogical thinking process — and consequently failed numerous times — with a fitness goal of mine.

I assumed it wouldn't take me more than 3 months to drop enough body fat to reach visible abs. After 3 months, I was still a long way from reaching the goal and I'd give up, frustrated that I hadn't achieved it. Looking back, it made no sense — even if it took me two years to achieve this goal, it would still be a success. I obsessed about the deadline, while in reality the *timeframe* wasn't important — reaching the goal was.

Try to focus on the tiny wins you get on a daily basis and remind yourself that even if you're crawling, you're still getting closer to your goal.

Obviously, if you have a goal that *must* be achieved by a certain date (such as preparing yourself for an important exam next week), this advice doesn't apply. Finishing your preparations for an exam a week after its date serves little to no purpose. If the deadline *is* key, slow progress can indeed make you fail. In such a case, apply the Ultimate Focus Strategy to the extreme: eliminate every single distraction and double down on your key objective to ensure that you reach it on time.

Usually deadline-oriented goals are relatively short-term, so it's possible to throw your life out of balance for a while to ensure that you accomplish the goal. Make sure it's an exception, though — living your life without balance in the long term brings more problems than benefits.

Another pitfall to avoid is comparing yourself to others and consequently becoming frustrated that, despite working so hard, you still can't match the performance of those other people.

Back in the day, when I started my journey with bodybuilding, I used to train with a friend. I came up with an idea to build a basement gym and researched what kind of equipment would be needed to perform an effective workout. I spent hours reading about nutrition and general fitness advice. I designed a workout plan and made sure we were performing the exercises properly.

Yet, despite me putting in so much effort, it was my friend — who often missed workouts, never read any articles about bodybuilding and fueled his workouts with Coke and potato chips — who transformed his body and looked like a person who actually went to the gym. Me? Even several years later, I still hadn't reached the physique my friend had developed within less than a year without putting much effort or making sacrifices.

Because of this experience of mine (and other similar experiences, too), I fully empathize with people who feel angry because no matter how hard they try, they still fail while others succeed with virtually no effort. Such apparent unfairness can understandably lead to discouragement.

I largely freed myself from feeling frustrated about it by making myself realize — and repeating it over and over in my head until it stuck — that life is *not* fair. Some people have it easier while some have it harder. Don't despair, though. It doesn't mean that some people suck at everything and some succeed with everything. All of us have a different set of strengths and weaknesses.

When I went to a trampoline park with my other friend (who's also my rock climbing partner) a couple of times, he was able to do a backflip during our second session. I, on the other hand — even after watching several detailed videos about how to perform a backflip and numerous attempts — couldn't do it.

On our last visit to the trampoline park, I actually performed it so badly while jumping into a foam pool that my shin hit against the hard, wooden edge of the pool. I still have the scar to remind me of the accident.

You could say, "That's so unfair. You clearly put more effort into it and you not only didn't succeed, but you also injured yourself." And you'd be right, except that when we go rock climbing, it's me who can naturally perform some moves that my friend can't. My and his strengths simply lie in different places.

When you feel frustrated that you're trying so hard but you still fail, remind yourself that there's probably another strength of yours that makes other people feel frustrated that it's so easy for you.

Another way to deal with this problem is to reframe your struggles. If you aren't good at something, you'll probably put more effort into it. Consequently, if you stick to it long enough, sooner or later you'll probably perform at least as well as the natural who seems to achieve everything so easily. Yes, you might suffer a lot during the process and it might take you a long time, but in the end, a weakness can be a blessing in disguise. Likewise, a natural strength — if you take it for granted — can be a curse.

I used to be an extremely insecure person with virtually non-existent social skills. Every naturally confident man always had it easier than me, but thanks to my effort and determination, I changed as a person and improved every aspect of my life. I'm not sure where I would be if it weren't for this "unfair" weakness that had crippled my life for so long.

Instead of merely relying on one's looks or natural social abilities, a shy person who is willing to change can eventually become a better "deal." Over the longer term, would an attractive woman interested in a serious relationship be more interested in a handsome "natural" who doesn't offer much substance beyond his looks and smooth talk, or a person who has invested years of his life to build confidence, develop powerful communication skills, and constantly improves himself?

EMPOWERING STORY #5: JIM PAUL

Ever since he was nine and got his first job as a caddy at a local golf club, Jim Paul knew that he would get rich. It wasn't important *how* he would do that; what was important was *how much*. As he used to say, "It wasn't what you did for a living that was important in life; it was how much you got paid for doing it.[27]"

Within the next three decades, he would go from being a nine-year-old making pennies to crossing $5,000, $10,000, $20,000, and $100,000 in daily earnings from successful trades.

He was making great money, spending most of his income on frivolous purchases, and living large, just like he had imagined as a nine-year-old caddy.

Deeply convinced of his trading abilities, in 1983 he bet it all on a speculation in the soybean market. Over the next few months, he would lose 1.6 million dollars — $400,000 of which he borrowed from friends.

Jim Paul spent the rest of the decade recovering from his failure. In his book, *What I Learned Losing a Million Dollars* (originally published in 1994), he admits responsibility for his failure and recounts lessons learned from this event that led him to an unsuccessful suicide attempt.

Most notably, he points out that, "Personalizing successes sets people up for disastrous failure. They begin to treat the success as a personal reflection, rather than the result of capitalizing on a good opportunity, being at the right place at the right time, or even being just plain lucky. People begin to think their mere involvement in the undertaking guarantees success.[28]"

Ultimately, overconfidence led Jim Paul to a spectacular failure. In the end, his failure taught him that he wasn't a good trader, and he had to relearn the profession with humility. He managed to recover from his failure and has helped thousands of investors avoid a similar financial catastrophe, thanks to sharing his own painful lessons in his book.

2. Failure because the process is unsustainable

If you're impatient, you're likely to set an unsustainable tempo from the get-go. While focusing on quick wins can work in the short term, burnout is almost guaranteed if you attempt to maintain a murderous tempo for a long period of time.

I know, I've been there many times.

I almost passed out in a sauna after neglecting my body's warning signals, and got nicely rewarded with a nasty case of the common cold. Prior to that event, I went to a sauna at least twice a month; now I stay away from it.

After months of sticking to a crazy routine of writing 3,000 words a day, I got burned out so much that merely thinking about writing made me feel like throwing up. My disgust was so strong I was afraid I would never be able to write again.

When I got into rock climbing, I was so impatient to improve that I repeatedly ripped off the callouses on my fingers. Then, instead of climbing hard on the next workout I either had to take a few days off to let my fingers heal a little or I needed to tape them to avoid further damage. I also had a finger tendon injury that resulted in a six-week break from climbing.

I won't lie. As unsustainable as some of my actions were, they helped me tremendously in the beginning. A short-term extreme approach can help, as long as you don't plan to maintain it forever. Your risk of burnout is relatively low during the first couple of weeks, and greatly increases with each additional week of increased tempo.

Writing 3,000 words a day meant that I could write several short books each month — and learn a lot from each one. A hard, no-excuse approach to exercising at the gym and climbing like a mad man with ripped callouses helped me get tougher. But in the end, I too had to transition into something more sustainable.

Now I write 1,000 words a day. That's a sustainable tempo that helps me achieve a lot without the risk of another burnout. Even if I believe I could write another 1,000 or 2,000 words, I stop myself right after accomplishing my daily word quota, because overextending myself on any given day can affect my sustainable routine.

I no longer practice several sports at once. I also pay more attention to proper recovery. Sometimes I take a few days off so that when I return my body is fully recharged. Then my performance is actually better than if I had continued working out with no such recovery period.

My hands got tougher and nowadays I rarely rip my skin off. However, I also pay close attention to my body's signals and back out whenever I feel there's an increased risk of an injury. Prioritizing long-term improvement over carelessly overtaxing my body leads to sustainable year-round progress.

If you frequently fail because you focus too much on the short-term unsustainable results, try to shift your outlook and embrace a long-term approach. Focus on building a chain of small improvements that you can make on a regular basis, rather than working yourself into the ground, deluding yourself that you can keep such a pace forever. As Zig Ziglar said, "It's not what you do every once in a while; it's what you do on a daily basis that makes the difference."

You can train extremely hard from time to time, but if you repeatedly overuse your body and never give it an opportunity to fully recover, there's a higher chance that you'll injure yourself, which won't improve your performance.

You can work 16-hour workdays every now and then if it's really needed, but if you do it consistently, the only reward you'll get will be lower creativity and overall lower productivity. In the end, instead of achieving more, you'll only achieve burnout, lose important relationships, and ruin your health.

Is it really worth it? More to the point, does it really get you to your goal?

There's a reason why the bodies of marathoners are completely different than the bodies of sprinters — you either focus on short bursts of high-intensity activity or you specialize in maintaining low-intensity activity over a long period of time.

If you're impatient by nature, I have bad news for you: most goals require the marathoner's approach. While you can kick things off with a short sprint, eventually you'll have to transition into a more sustainable tempo and temper your impetuousness.

If I were to offer you two investments — one with a 20% return and another with a 7% return — which would you choose? Obviously, you'd go with the former, wouldn't you? 20% is better than 7%.

What if I told you that the 20% return comes with a 20% risk of losing all of your money while the 7% return comes with a 1% risk of this unfavorable scenario?

In probability theory, expected value (EV) is the sum of all possible values for a random variable, each multiplied by its probability of occurrence. Poker players use EV to calculate their expected profit and make mathematically correct bets. You can use it to make better long-term decisions.[29]

20% risk doesn't sound that bad, does it? Let's calculate the expected value for an investment of $1,000 and see if it's a good approach.

With the first option, 20% of the time you'd lose $1000 and 80% of the time you'd make $200. Let's calculate the EV:

20% x ($1000) = ($200)

80% x $200 = $160

($200) + $160 = ($40)

EV = -$40

A negative EV means that over the long run you're guaranteed to lose more than you would gain. Whenever you're choosing fast, unsustainable results, you're going with the risky option — and now you have the math to prove it. Your potential returns are higher, but in the long term, it's a bad bet because eventually you're guaranteed to lose.

Now let's compare it with the safer option of the 7% return with a 1% risk.

1% of the time you'd lose $1000 and 99% of the time you'd make $70.

1% x ($1000) = ($10)

99% x $70 = $69.3

($10) + $69.3 = $59.3

EV = $59.3

A positive EV means that over the long run you're mathematically guaranteed to win, and that's the investment option you should choose, despite 20% returns sounding much more attractive. This is how maintaining a sustainable tempo works in the long term. It might not be as glamorous as working yourself to bone, but it's what produces consistent results.

DEALING WITH A FAILURE DUE TO IMPATIENCE: QUICK RECAP

1. People often fail because they're impatient. They'll either give up, frustrated by the slow progress, or they'll set an unsustainable tempo, anxious to succeed as quickly as possible. In both cases, failure is more likely than success.

2. If you often fail because slow progress discourages you, focus on reaching the goal itself, not on reaching it within a made-up deadline. Deadlines should be rough estimates; they can't dictate your life.

Be careful not to compare yourself to others or get angry that you fail while others succeed. You might not be as good as others in one thing, but outperform them in something else. Also, if you have it harder, you'll most likely put more effort into it. Over the long term, you have a high chance of outperforming the ones who take their talents for granted.

3. If you fail because you're so anxious to reach your goal that you follow an unsustainable routine, understand the difference between sprinting and marathoning.

A brief sprint might be extremely helpful to gain initial momentum with a new goal. Here's the thing, though: it needs to be a *brief* sprint, not a long-term strategy.

After a certain period of time (such as a few weeks, or perhaps a few months), you need to transition into a more sustainable routine, particularly for big goals that take years to achieve. In the end, it's all about what you do on a *daily* basis, not every now and then. Little steps made daily and consistently are better than crash and burn undertakings.

Chapter 8: Dealing With a Failure Due to Self-Licensing

One of the most interesting concepts in social psychology is the subconscious phenomenon of self-licensing, in which a person's increased confidence in their positive image makes them more likely to engage in immoral or negative behaviors.[30] As scientists put it, "Past good deeds can liberate individuals to engage in behaviors that are immoral, unethical, or otherwise problematic."

For example, a person who drinks diet soda will discount the high caloric content of a pizza or cheeseburger. The diet soda gives them a moral license to gorge on fast food — after all, it's *diet* soda, right?

You financially support pro-environment causes and then drive a huge gas-guzzling SUV to a store two minutes away. You gulp down a multivitamin and a few supplements — and then proceed to eat empty calories. You buy energy-efficient lights or appliances and then use them more carelessly than before, which in the end increases your energy use.

Let's address some common goals you might fail to achieve because of self-licensing:

1. Exercise and weight loss

I have a friend who exercises every now and then. He spends an hour or so in the gym, and then, having obtained a moral license, drives to the store to buy a sugary post-workout yogurt drink or to a fast food restaurant to have a "post-workout" meal.

It's a classic case of taking one step forward and two steps back. People vastly overestimate the amount of calories they burn when exercising, and what they consider a harmless tasty reward after a workout sets them back. In fact, a small study suggests that people believe they burn three to four times more calories during exercise and then end up eating two to three times more calories than they burned during the exercise.[31]

Calorie-wise, it would have been better not to exercise at all than to exercise and then more than recoup the burned calories with a post-workout cheat meal. However, in addition to its potential weight loss benefits, exercise is important for overall health. The solution is not to stop exercising, but to educate yourself about energy expenditure during exercise and become more conscious of your post-workout food choices.

Self-licensing will make you feel as if you've "earned" your calories. You exercised so hard, burned *at least* 1000 calories, so go on, grab a cheeseburger and some fries and feel good about how active and healthy a person you are. In reality, you may have burned 300 calories and even a single cheeseburger would more than offset what you've just burned.

If you want to lose weight, make sure that the caloric content of a post-workout meal is lower than your energy expenditure during the exercise. Considering that you need a deficit of 3500 calories to lose a pound of fat, you need to maintain a daily deficit of at least 500 calories to lose a pound a week. It's tough to train your way to a slim body, and I'll show you why with a little game.

How many calories does an average adult burn during one hour of brisk walking?

600, 400, or 200?

The correct answer is "about 200." Eat a single banana as your "post-workout" meal and you're down to about 100 calories burned. Eat it with some yogurt and you've just consumed more calories than you burned during exercise. Walk at a slower pace instead of walking briskly and a single banana will wipe out any caloric deficit.

How about one hour of jogging? It burns about 400 calories. One large slice of pizza is enough to cancel out the burned calories. And show me a person who eats just *one* slice of pizza when they're hungry after exercise!

That's why a moral license to reward yourself with a post-workout meal is so dangerous. Exercise alone rarely, if ever, is sufficient to lose weight. It's essential to cut down your daily calorie intake and be aware that a moral license that you obtain from exercising can actually hinder your weight loss.

2. Health

Wherever in the world you are, a local supermarket will most likely have at least one aisle with "healthy" food. Purchasing some "healthy" snacks gives you a license to indulge in your favorite, less than healthy foods, because "Hey, look at me! My shopping cart is filled to the brim with stuff labeled (by the manufacturer) as healthy."

In the end, most of what people consider "healthy" food isn't actually all that healthy or still needs to be consumed in moderation. Brown sugar is still sugar. Nuts are rich in minerals and vitamins, but when you add heaps of salt and artificial flavorings, they don't differ much from junk food. Whole-grain graham crackers are still low in nutrients. Pure squeezed orange juice is still full of fructose and lacks the dietary fiber you can find in an orange.

Be skeptical when it comes to food labeled as healthy and stick to what humans have been eating forever, particularly vegetables and fruits. As a rule of thumb, listen to Michael Pollan, author of *Food Rules: An Eater's Manual*, and avoid food with more than five ingredients, ingredients you can't pronounce, or anything your great grandmother wouldn't recognize as food.

3. Personal finances

Self-licensing makes it easy to overspend.

You buy energy-efficient lights and then don't bother to turn them off — after all, they're energy-efficient, right? Then the energy bill comes and you need to pay more than before installing the new lights.

You see a great deal in the store — buy a $100 block knife set for just $75 and you'll get a free bowl set. Proud of how much money you've saved, you get back home and realize your old knives are perfectly sharp and you don't need any kitchen bowls.

When you save money, self-licensing might tempt you to overspend on your next purchase — after all, you've saved a few bucks, so it won't hurt to spend a little more. You'll still be ahead, right? Just like in the example with weight loss, in the end you'll probably more than make up for the money you saved originally by making additional unnecessary purchases.

I strongly suggest automating your finances as much as you can to reduce the dangers of overspending with a moral license.

Set up an automatic weekly or monthly bank transfer of a portion of your income to another bank account where you only hold your savings. If you receive an unexpected amount of money or save a considerable sum by avoiding an expense, immediately send it to this account as well.

The more difficult it is to take out your savings (but without the risk of losing principal — this is about building an emergency fund you *can* access relatively quickly if needed), the more effective this strategy will be. Out of sight, out of mind.

You can also set a low spending limit on your credit card. Obviously, you can always change these limits, but an additional step preventing you from carelessly spending money might be enough to stop you in your tracks.

If the ease of a paying with a credit card is what challenges your willpower the most, get rid of your credit cards. Replace them with debit cards that draw money directly out of your own bank account. That way, you won't be able to easily go over your budget.

Last but not least, consider paying in cash. It's harder to part with money if you physically hand it over to a cashier instead of swiping a piece of plastic. Paying with cash makes you more conscious of what lands in your shopping cart and whether you really need it. It's more difficult to fall victim to self-licensing if you physically need to part ways with cold, hard cash.

Avoid Self-Licensing With This Mindset Change

If you're about to do something you tell yourself you've *earned the right to do* just because you did something that you consider *good*, it's probably bad for you. Compensating good behaviors with bad behaviors is not a sustainable strategy to reach your goals.

The most problematic situation leading to failure is following positive habits with negative rewards. Thinking in terms of entitlement — I *deserve* a reward because I performed this positive habit — is a sure-fire way to engage in self-licensing.

The positive activity in which you engage should be your reward in itself. If there's no need for a reward afterwards, there's no risk of overcompensation.

For example, when I eat a healthy salad, I don't feel the need to eat junk food afterwards because I *love* the flavor of salad. I don't eat a salad just so I can get permission to eat something unhealthy. The salad is a reward in itself.

Granted, this is only possible if you actually enjoy the positive habits in which you engage. If you go to the gym to do exercises you hate because you *must* exercise, there's no wonder you feel the need to reward yourself after your workout. Find a different way to engage in physical activity that will be a reward in itself and you'll avoid the negative effects of self-licensing.

As a final suggestion and a general rule of thumb, be vigilant whenever an act of self-improvement inflates your self-image. It's easy to do stupid things when you feel you're the smartest person in the world.

DEALING WITH A FAILURE DUE TO SELF-LICENSING: QUICK RECAP

1. Self-licensing is a phenomenon in which a person who engaged in a good behavior is more likely to engage in a negative behavior, overcompensating for past good deeds with things that are bad for them.

2. In weight loss, pay close attention to what you eat after exercise. Ideally, consider physical activity a reward in itself so that you won't have a tendency to think you've "earned" junk food. Most people vastly overestimate the amount of calories they burn during the workout. They end up eating more than they need, which makes exercise contribute to weight *gain* instead of weight *loss*.

3. When it comes to health, be skeptical about "healthy" foods. Just because the food is in the "healthy" aisle or comes with "healthy" labels, doesn't mean it's actually healthy for you. And even if it indeed is, be cautious not to overcompensate for your healthy choices by throwing a bag of chips (or two) into your shopping cart. As with exercise, engaging in a positive habit doesn't mean you've earned the right to engage in a negative behavior.

4. In finance, be aware that whenever you make a good financial decision, you might be tempted to reward yourself with an unnecessary purchase. Be particularly cautious about discounts that make you feel you're a smart shopper, when in fact you stock up on items you don't need. To protect yourself against self-licensing, automate your finances — set up automatic monthly transfers to save

at least a small portion of your income. Setting low spending limits on your credit card or paying with a debit card or cash instead might also prove helpful.

5. As a rule of thumb, remember that if you're about to do something you believe you've *earned the right to do*, it's probably bad for you. Whenever you compensate for good behaviors with negative habits, you're taking one step forward and two steps back. Make sure that you actually *enjoy* your positive habits. Then just engaging in them will be a sufficient reward for you.

6. Lastly, question your decisions when you've recently inflated your self-image by making a good decision, such as eating a healthy salad (that can make you feel like you can now eat a chocolate bar), exercising (by rewarding yourself with more calories than you burned), or finding a good deal (so now you can reward yourself with that gizmo you wouldn't otherwise buy).

PART 2:
5 Rules and Exercises to Develop and Maintain a Success-Friendly Mindset

I decided to end 2016 with one more uncomfortable challenge: a 3-day water fast.

Prior to coming up with this idea, the longest I went without food was about 40 hours — and 40 hours without food isn't as challenging as one might think. You only skip one full day of eating, and if you're busy the entire day, you hardly notice it.

A 3-day fast was something different. I decided that I wouldn't eat anything on the 28th, 29th, and 30th of December.

People asked me why I would do such a thing. What's the point of willingly experiencing such discomfort? Wasn't it dangerous? Wouldn't my muscles break down? Wouldn't I faint or spend entire days dreaming about food? My answer — regardless of what crazy idea I come up with — is always the same: if you want to grow as a person, you need to challenge yourself.

It's one of my most important personal rules. I believe it's one of the key differences between people who realize their full potential and people who succumb to mediocrity and go through life never feeling entirely fulfilled or satisfied.

Yes, I may suffer because of my experiments, but there's meaning in this suffering: I grow as a person and learn new lessons.

In the end, my fasting challenge turned out to be a non-event. It wasn't that much harder to go without food for three days as it is to go without food for 40 hours. Still, it was an interesting lesson and a new challenge I could add to my ever-growing collection of weird experiments. Now I know that if I were ever forced to go without food for three days, I wouldn't suffer much.

In this part of the book, each chapter will discuss a different rule to help you develop a success-friendly mindset. I will accompany each principle with an exercise to introduce it in your everyday life.

Please note that all of these rules are based on my personal experience and worldview. I don't claim to know all the answers, so please treat my suggestions as what they are — *suggestions*. If a different rule works better for you, stick to it. You know yourself best. What's more important than following my exact rules is to have *some* success-friendly rules that you follow in your life; they will help you maintain consistent habits and cultivate your core values.

Chapter 9: You Must Live Your Life the Hard Way and Regularly Embrace Uncertainty

At the moment I'm writing this paragraph, in an hour I need to leave for a close-quarters combat krav maga seminar. It will be a three-hour long training, covering situations such as being assaulted by an attacker with a firearm or being taken hostage.

I've never attended such a seminar and I feel apprehensive about it. However, if years of embracing uncertainty have taught me something, is that whenever you feel uncertain about something, it's most likely going to help you grow a lot.

I opened my first book, *How to Build Self-Discipline: Resist Temptations and Reach Your Long-Term Goals*, with a prologue titled, "Life Is Easy When You Live It the Hard Way."

The words come from Kekich's Credos, 100 rules developed by longevity scientist David Kekich. The entire credo is as follows: "Real regrets only come from not doing your best. All else is out of your control. You're measured by results only. Trade excuses and 'trying' for results, and expect half-hearted results from half-hearted efforts. Do more than is expected of you. Life's easy when you live it the hard way... and hard if you try to live it the easy way."

This rule is one of the key elements of my decision-making process. Even if I often hate myself for putting myself in so much stress and discomfort, I know that in the long term, the stress I'm willingly learning to handle today will turn me into a stronger person.

One of my favorite quotes related to this concept comes from Arnold Schwarzenegger, who said: "Strength does not come from winning. Your struggles develop your strengths. When you go through hardships and decide not to surrender, that is strength."

No matter if you're old or young, male or female, living in North America, South America, Europe, Africa, Asia, Australia, or Antarctica, when you deliberately live your life the hard way, you *will* get stronger, and this will help you push through failures and achieve the success you want.

However, please note that we're talking about *voluntary, self-imposed* discomfort. People living in war zones might be the most resilient individuals in the world, but I don't wish upon them — or anyone, for that matter — to suffer such a horrible situation unwillingly. Expanding your comfort zone *voluntarily* will help you handle non-voluntary circumstances. Hopefully these future difficult moments won't be a matter of life or death, but will merely be about whether you accomplish your goal or not.

Driving back home from the krav maga seminar, I realized that the anxiety you feel prior to leaving your comfort zone often overplays what's going to happen in reality.

I was afraid I'd be the only one without a military background in a group of highly-trained people who *did* have a military background. I was afraid I'd have a reckless sparring partner who wouldn't care if he injured me during the training. I was afraid the hostage situation simulation would be traumatic.

In the end, none of those things happened. Okay, with the exception of the latter. I suppose that lying on your stomach with your hands zip-tied, a garbage bag on your head, a tape on your mouth, and gasping for air counts as traumatic. And due to practicing how to escape from zip ties, for a few days my hands looked as if I had spent a weekend in a sadomasochist dungeon.

However, none of this was even close to what I was afraid of. The next time I participate in such an event (or anything similar, for that matter), I won't be even half as stressed by it as I was before my first seminar.

That's precisely why regularly embracing uncertainty is so important for success. By continuously expanding your comfort zone, fewer and fewer unknown things in life will scare you. You'll be well-equipped to face any discomforts with a calm attitude. You might even welcome them because of the growth they have given you in the past.

As performance coach Tony Robbins once said, "The quality of your life is in direct proportion to the amount of uncertainty you can comfortably live with. The more uncertainty you can live with, the more you'll try, the more you'll learn, the more alive you'll be. The more you got to be certain about everything, the less you'll have."[32]

EXERCISE #7: LIVING LIFE THE HARD WAY

A misattributed Eleanor Roosevelt quote (it was actually said by the Chicago Tribune journalist Mary Schmich[33]) says: "Do one thing every day that scares you." I'd add to that: "or makes you uncomfortable."

It's a great piece of advice, if not slightly unrealistic. You have a life to live, and obviously you won't always have time, energy, or means of doing something that scares you or makes you uncomfortable.

However, no matter how busy you are, you can probably turn it into a weekly exercise. At the beginning of each week, come up with at least one thing that scares you or makes you uncomfortable and do it during the week.

All levels of fear and discomfort count. — you don't have to jump out of an airplane on a weekly basis. It can be something more mundane, which still generates some fear, anxiety, or discomfort. The more often you perform this exercise, the better. When you deliberately make your life harder, it becomes easier.

For example, at the time of writing this, yesterday I sent out a sales message I was slightly afraid to send out. Two days ago, I had a climbing workout, and those — as much as I love them — always produce some fear or discomfort. Three days before that, I attended the close-quarters combat krav maga seminar.

In any given year, I probably engage in well over 100 scary situations with a varying level of discomfort. This self-imposed connection to fear and discomfort keeps me on my toes. I can never get too complacent and slip into easy living because there's always a new fear- or discomfort-producing activity coming soon. I'm aware that this might sound like hell if you love to stay comfortable, but just imagine how extremely comfortable I feel coming back home from another crazy adventure!

The next time you feel uncertain or afraid of something, tell yourself you need to do it precisely because you're afraid. There's no shame or failure in feeling fear or uncertainty. It's only when you decide against doing something out of fear that you suffer a great loss — a loss of a powerful learning opportunity.

Obviously, this is not about being stupid and doing things that can potentially harm you or kill you. Granted, there's often *some* risk, but that's why you need to make a calculated decision. As scary as it looks, there's very little risk in skydiving in tandem with an experienced skydiver. But there is a lot of risk (or rather, stupidity) in cliff jumping when you're unsure about the water's depth and the potential obstacles it contains.

When I climb a difficult route, I'll keep pushing despite my fear, as long as I know that a potential fall is likely to be safe. If I'm about to climb into a so-called "no-fall zone" wherein a fall can have disastrous consequences due to sparse protection or a certain feature of a rock, I make a calculated decision based on how I feel about the chances of success and the risk of falling off. This is *not* a time to mindlessly follow the "I'm afraid, so I need to do it" approach!

Keep that in mind whenever you find yourself in such a situation. This book is presented solely for motivational and informational purposes and I'm not responsible for your choices, but I care about you and want you to take risks as safely as possible. Some of the safe or relatively safe risks you can play with to embrace more uncertainty in your life include:

- any type of an extreme sport or activity done with or supervised by an experienced professional. This includes skydiving in tandem, hot air ballooning, white water rafting, bungee jumping, hang gliding, surfing, or mountain biking. Note that you'll never be 100% safe when doing extreme sports, but practicing them with proper supervision greatly reduces the risk.

- approaching that attractive man or woman. There's virtually no physical risk here (unless you have the bad luck of running into a jealous boyfriend or girlfriend), but it comes with a level of fear that can paralyze you even more than an extreme sport.

- public speaking. Another type of an activity that comes with pretty much zero physical risk (okay, you can fall off the stage if you're not careful), but still generates incredible amounts of fear and anxiety — and consequently, a lot of learning opportunities.

- traveling to an exotic country. As long as you do due diligence and avoid places that *are* indeed unsafe, traveling poses virtually no danger while it exposes you to character-shaping discomfort.

YOU MUST LIVE YOUR LIFE THE HARD WAY AND REGULARLY EMBRACE UNCERTAINTY: QUICK RECAP

1. You must live your life the hard way and regularly embrace uncertainty. The quality of your life depends on how good you are at handling fear and uncertainty, so make sure that you don't avoid discomfort. Putting yourself in such situations isn't always fun, but it's one of the best ways to attract more success into your life.

2. Try to engage in uncomfortable or scary situations at least once a week. This will help you toughen up and prepare you to handle any unforeseen difficulties in a calm manner.

Chapter 10: You Must Show the Middle Finger to Your Ego

We've already discussed that people go to great lengths to avoid suffering a blow to their ego.

I say, "Screw that!" Show the middle finger to your ego and don't be afraid to look ridiculous in front of others. During the close-quarters combat seminar, we practiced escaping from zip ties by performing a rapid downwards motion. To my surprise, I succeeded on my first try. But then I failed every single time after that, flailing my arms like a crazy chicken (to the great joy of my sparring partner, who exploded with laughter after each of my failures).

Fortunately, I had trained myself a long time ago to not care about such situations. I rarely, if ever, feel self-conscious when I fall on my butt or do something stupid. I'm a newbie, so it's obvious I'm going to fail and look ridiculous. Not trying your best merely because you don't want to look stupid in front of other people is what I consider truly stupid.

Adhering to this principle means that you don't feel guilty or inferior because you can't yet do something . As we've already discussed, failure is necessary in order to learn. The ones who care about their *progress* and not about their image are the ones who learn the most quickly.

In my climbing gym, I sometimes see new climbers who are so protective of their ego that the moment they fall off a route, they look around (obviously embarrassed), worried that somebody saw them fall. Then they give up and move on to climb something easier.

I shudder to think about all the horrible things that would happen if somebody saw them fall again. Can't have that. Their egos are more important than learning, right? I don't claim to be better than them. It took me years to battle my own embarrassment and feel good, even when looking stupid. I know it's a difficult process, and I greatly admire those who decide to push their egos aside and keep trying.

EXERCISE #8: TRY AGAIN

If you have a tendency to protect your ego by avoiding looking silly when you are learning something new, expose yourself to as many such situations as you can — and simply try again instead of worrying about what others think of you.

Try to catch yourself each time you're worried that you look stupid and shift your attention back to the task you're trying to master. Let me assure you that nobody cares about your failures as much as you think. When you're worried about others laughing at your clumsy attempts, they're often equally worried that they look silly in your eyes!

Don't Take Yourself So Seriously

The more seriously you take yourself, the more difficult life will get for you. Protecting your ego will not only make you less likely to try again after a failure, it will also bring unnecessary frustration.

A couple of days ago, when learning basic Russian, I made an embarrassing mistake during a class with my teacher. Dwelling on it would only cause me unnecessary suffering and possibly affect my learning speed. Laughing at how embarrassing it was — and even sharing the story with other people and making them laugh at my expense — helped me quickly forget about it and move on.

Whenever you feel embarrassed about a failure, try to find something funny in it. Laughing it off will help you process it more quickly than if you were to waste time worrying about your image or constantly picturing the situation in your head and reliving the embarrassment over and over again.

EMPOWERING STORY #6: ARNO ILGNER

Arno Ilgner established himself as a bold rock climber who put up with scary and dangerous routes. Recognition fueled his sense of superiority, but deep down he went through long periods of times when he felt inferior.

As he recalls in his book, *The Rock Warrior's Way: Mental Training for Climbers*, "I was caught in an external value system which forced me to see myself as either better than or worse than others. I compared my externals to the externals of others, concocting weak schemes why I was more or less valuable than someone else."[34]

He recounts a situation in which he approached a difficult route with his usual cockiness. However, this time the route he considered to be within his capabilities defeated him and he took a fall. Arno was embarrassed by his failure. Upon seeing some friends scrambling up in their direction, he asked his belayer not to tell them that he fell. To Arno, admitting a failure was equal to being inferior, and he would rather lie to his friends than admit his defeat.

It would take him until age 35 to go beyond the idea that self-worth isn't defined by failure or success. Inspired primarily by the works of Carlos Castaneda, he discovered that self-worth comes from an internal value system, and not merely from an achievement. Upon this realization, he developed his own system of mental training for rock climbing.

In *The Rock Warrior's Way*, he teaches that "If you want a more consistent and authentic source from which to draw a sense of self-worth and personal power, you will eventually need to reject external factors, such as comparison and achievement. You must look inside and embrace learning."

The concept of prioritizing learning over the ego became one of the basic tenets of his climbing philosophy that is now being taught in the United States, Mexico, Brazil and Spain.

YOU MUST SHOW THE MIDDLE FINGER TO YOUR EGO: QUICK RECAP

1. Show the middle finger to your ego. A fear of embarrassment should be the last thing on your mind when you're learning something new. If you don't try again because you're afraid of looking stupid, that's when you actually exhibit an unintelligent behavior.

2. Don't take your embarrassing failures seriously. Laughing them off will help you process them quickly, while dwelling on them and worrying about your image will only prolong the suffering.

Chapter 11: You Must Feel Worthy of Success

People who don't believe they deserve success rarely achieve it — or if they do, they'll subconsciously sabotage their efforts so they can go back to the previous state of things.

There are two main causes of this destructive belief:

1. You don't want to hurt others

You're such a loving person that you feel it's unfair when you reach success and others don't. I don't mean this in a sarcastic sense — some people *do* limit their growth because they don't want to outdo their family members or friends.

When you excel in several walks of life and other people around you struggle, it's understandable you might feel guilty or at least uncomfortable about the divide between you and others. However, these emotions and worries are unfounded; by reaching success, you'll benefit the world more than by deliberately limiting your achievements.

For example, if you built a successful business and your friend is struggling to pay their bills, you'd be able to give them pointers on how to start a small business or even loan them some money to get started. If you lost weight and your friend is struggling to get in shape, you'd be able to help them by becoming their accountability partner. Your parents will probably be proud of you when you outdo them. After all, almost every parent wants their children to have the best life possible.

Convert your feelings of love into inspiration to keep growing, as this will enable you to help others even more. As such a caring person, you're more than worthy of success and will do a lot of good when you turn your dreams into reality.

2. You don't recognize your strengths

In my books, I generally don't talk about low self-esteem because I'm not as qualified to do justice to this topic as a professional therapist would be. For the purpose of this chapter, I'm only going to address the possible situation in which you consider yourself *inadequate* to achieve success, but otherwise don't suffer from a lack of self-esteem. If you do lack self-esteem in most aspects of your life, that condition requires professional care, so please consult a qualified expert.

I used to doubt my worth and abilities. Why would *I* reach success? What is so special about me that, out of so many people in the world, I am the one who can make his dreams happen? What makes *me* think that after so many failures, I'd be able to convert them into success?

The process that helped me overcome my negative thought processes was inspired by Tony Robbins' books, *Unlimited Power* and *Awaken the Giant Within*. The idea is that you can't get past negative thoughts unless you access a more resourceful state of mind. In essence, you're seeking reasons why you *can* do something instead of worrying that you can't do it — something we've already talked about at the beginning of the book.

EXERCISE #9: MINING FOR RESOURCES

Here are three very effective questions that will help you recognize your strengths and instruct your brain to think in a more constructive way. Be as detailed as possible when answering these questions, as this process can help you greatly in overcoming your self-limiting beliefs.

1. What are the reasons why it's so important to you that you'll achieve your goal?

This primarily comes down to your inner motivation — the reasons why you absolutely *must* achieve this goal. That's why it's so crucial to have goals that fire you up. Otherwise, it's hard to gather enough confidence to make them happen.

If possible, I strongly suggest coming up with reasons that go beyond yourself. For example, my most important motivation to succeed in business was to help my parents build a house in the countryside. This one reason alone was sufficient to keep me going and maintain my confidence, no matter how much failure I suffered.

Spend a lot of time writing down your answers to this question. The more powerful your reasons are, the easier it will be to boost your confidence. As we've already discussed, if you don't believe in yourself, you need to at least believe in the importance of the goal you want to achieve.

2. What are your unique strengths or resources that will help you reach your goal?

Name your top strengths that you can apply to your goal. Are you stubborn? Do you have a lot of self-discipline? Are you persistent? Are you generally a positive person? Do you have integrity? Are you a great communicator? Do you speak foreign languages? Do you think big? Are you well-organized? Passionate? Patient? Curious? Enthusiastic?

Imagine that you have a job interview for a company called Your Goal, Inc. How would you sell yourself in order to be hired for that position?

Come up with personal skills and traits, as well as other resources that can help you achieve your objective. These can be something like access to a network of people who've already achieved your goal, money, specific knowledge, stable job, equipment, and other assets, such as a strong support circle, well-stocked library, paid-off house, high energy, or strong health.

3. When and how did you use your strengths or resources to achieve your previous goals?

You've already jotted down your unique strengths and resources. Now it's time to think of past situations in which you used your strengths or resources. The goal is to realize that you've already successfully tapped into your inner resourcefulness in the past, so now you can do it again.

Let's imagine you want to find a better job. A few years ago, you started jogging, and you continue this routine to this day. If you're so self-disciplined as to exercise regularly over a long period of time, why wouldn't you be able to apply your self-discipline to a consistent, determined job search?

If you're a caring person who's always there for their family and friends, this means you can extend this nurturing aspect of your personality to yourself. If you're always there to help others overcome challenges in their lives, why wouldn't you be able to use it to reach your goals, too?

It doesn't have to be anything big. Even if it's something as ordinary as never being late to work or always making your bed in the morning, it still speaks of your positive traits that can help you reach your goal. A punctual person is essentially a person who sticks to their promises, while a person who always makes their bed in the morning is most likely organized and meticulous.

Alternatively, in place of answering these three questions, answer just this one question: "Why are you strong?" People often tend to focus on their weaknesses and reasons why they aren't worthy of success instead of coming up with reasons why they *do* deserve it. There's strength in all of us, but not all of us have discovered it yet.

When you make an extensive list of reasons *why* you're strong — and this can include everything from the fact that you're a loving person, you're punctual, you have integrity, you value education, or you think big — you'll bring to light your true, inner confidence. Whenever you feel doubtful, re-read your list until you can quote it from memory.

Don't expect that this exercise will magically make you a super confident person overnight, though. Its purpose is to get you to stop doubting yourself so much and think in a more constructive way by identifying real-world resources that can help you to achieve your goal. Only then can you successfully begin working on your goal.

YOU MUST FEEL WORTHY OF SUCCESS: QUICK RECAP

1. If you don't believe you deserve success, you'll sabotage your efforts. If you limit your growth because you're afraid of hurting others, remind yourself that becoming a better person gives you more resources to help them.

2. If you don't recognize your strengths, make a list of your motivations, strengths, relationships, and other assets that can help you achieve your goal. Then think of past situations that you solved, thanks to these resources.

Chapter 12: You Must Take Personal Responsibility

In one of the previous chapters I mentioned the concept of *locus of control*.

Locus of control is the degree to which people believe that they have control over the outcome of events in their lives. It can be internal (you'll blame yourself for your failures and praise yourself for your successes), or it can be external (you'll believe that things just happen to you and that you can't shape your future).

In other words, you either take the ship's wheel and assume responsibility for what happens, or let the ship drift and hope the ocean will steer you in the right direction. I don't think I need to tell you which approach is success-friendly!

Studies suggest that people with an external locus of control are more likely to suffer from stress or depression.[35] The more external their locus is, the greater the depression. After all, how can you be optimistic if you believe that you're at the mercy of fate, luck, or politicians?

Ralph Waldo Emerson once said, "Shallow men believe in luck or in circumstance. Strong men believe in cause and effect." When you consider every failure or success as an effect of your own decision, you acknowledge responsibility for your life and consequently, gain more control over it.

The concept of locus of control is related to *learned helplessness*, in which a person accepts that they have lost control and gives up trying to change the situation in which they find themselves.[36] If you repeatedly fail an exam, you may come to a conclusion that you're incapable of improving your performance and stop trying to succeed. What follows is the belief that events in your life are uncontrollable and, without taking personal responsibility, you'll never learn from any failure.

EXERCISE #10: ACKNOWLEDGING RESPONSIBILITY

If you want to develop a healthy internal locus of control and overcome learned helplessness, it's important to acknowledge responsibility for your life.

1. The first step is to make a list of past events that you *did* affect with your direct actions. Research suggests that increasing your awareness of previous experiences in which you were able to affect the outcome can help you immunize yourself against the belief that things are uncontrollable.[37]

This works in the exact same way as the "D" step (Dispute the Belief) of the A-B-C-D-E process of reversing limiting beliefs developed by positive psychologist Martin Seligman.[38] The idea is to come up with at least one piece of evidence against your belief so that you can point out that this belief is inaccurate. Suddenly "Things are beyond my control" can turn into "Things are *sometimes* beyond my control," and that makes a world of difference in how you perceive your control over life.

2. Next, write down a list of past failures that you blame on external factors. Try to find at least one action of yours that might have contributed to the situation, so you can see that it wasn't entirely caused by something beyond your control.

For example, if you have trouble losing weight but you always blame it on your genes or your friends who tempt you to eat junk food, was there at least *one* situation in which you could have easily refused the temptation but succumbed to it anyway? I know I found myself in many such situations. As much as I would have *loved* to not be responsible for my being overweight many years ago, I know I contributed at least partly to the situation, so things weren't entirely beyond my control.

Now, please note that I don't want you to beat yourself up for every failure. It's important to exhibit self-compassion instead of self-guilt. Also, please note that you shouldn't take ownership of a failure that clearly wasn't caused by you. If your ex left you because they found somebody else, don't shop for pain by thinking about what you did wrong, because maybe you didn't do *anything* wrong. Things like that do happen.

Acknowledge responsibility for things that were indeed at least partly within your control. For example, if you used to shout at and disrespect your ex, then yes, it might have been caused by you. If not, heed the Stoic advice and accept that it's no longer up to you, as painful and difficult as that might be.

3. The third step addresses the future or present situations you believe are beyond your control. Overcome passive acceptance and take personal responsibility by writing down a list of possible choices and options to handle the situation. When you're done, go through your ideas one by one and choose the best course of action.

We've already discussed that even if many things are beyond your control, you can *always* control your emotional responses. If you *really* don't have any other choices, at least you have a choice to think about the situation in a different way, and that can often produce a breakthrough.

Even if your list only has a few items on it, it still serves as evidence that in the end you *do* have some control over what happens.

4. The last step is simple, but can produce profound changes: eliminate phrases like "I have no choice" from your vocabulary.

Instead of saying that you have no choice, you can say, "I don't like my choices, but I choose to..." Maybe your options aren't ideal, but you can always choose *something* — and making this choice shows that you assume responsibility for the situation. In the end, remember that *not* making a choice is also a choice — and often, the worst one.

YOU MUST TAKE PERSONAL RESPONSIBILITY: QUICK RECAP

1. You must take personal responsibility for every success and failure. In scientific terms, it's called having an internal locus of control, and it's a trait shared by all successful people.

2. Shift your locus of control from external to internal by: increasing your awareness of previous experiences over which you exerted control; finding at least one past action of yours that could have contributed to a failure you believed was caused by external factors; coming up with choices and options that will affect a current or future challenge (to remind yourself that you *do* have some control); and lastly, eliminate phrases like "I have no choice" from your vocabulary.

Chapter 13: You Must Identify What You Want — And Go After It

I have important news to share with you: so far, scientists haven't figured out how to reverse death. It sucks, I know. Unfortunately, we all have an expiration date, so wouldn't it be nice to make the most out of our life while we're still here? Here's where the last rule comes into play.

The ultimate failure in life is not going after the things you want. If you don't *actively* identify what you want and then go after it, it will be "fate" or other people that will control your life. Let me assure you that it won't be even a tenth as much fun as writing your own script.

Realize that if you don't have a clear vision of your life, you'll never be able to recognize:

- when the right opportunity appears right in front of you;

- when a key person who can help you achieve your goals enters your life; or

- when the circumstances align in such a way that you'd be able to take advantage of them and produce a breakthrough.

In the end, if you don't know what you want, you won't be able to identify what can help you get it, and consequently, you'll be unlikely to ever achieve the success you crave.

Let me share with you a personal story that might look like I got lucky, but in fact it happened as a result of clearly knowing what I wanted.

After one of my businesses failed because the business model didn't fit my personality, I realized I had to get more specific about the kind of a business I wanted to own. I told myself that it would have to be an online business that wouldn't require me to hire employees and that I wouldn't have to be managing it on a daily basis by taking calls, writing emails, and so on.

Somehow I heard about this thing called self-publishing, where you could write books, publish them online and people from all over the world could buy them with a click of a mouse. And there were even some people making great money with this business model!

As if by magic, I stumbled upon a forum thread in which a successful self-published author offered some tips. Having identified that his business model might be a great fit for me, I reached out to him to ask if he offered coaching.

Yet again I was "lucky," because he was just about to launch a new course and I could join as one of the early adopters. Back then, it was by far the most expensive digital product I'd ever bought. Fortunately, I managed to scrape together enough savings to purchase it and began my education. The rest is history.

The most important lesson here is that I knew what specifically I wanted to achieve and went after it when the opportunity presented itself. It wasn't any magical force that created the new opportunities and brought the right person in my life; by clearly knowing what I wanted, I could take advantage of the opportunities I would otherwise overlook. Who knows, maybe during this time I also rubbed elbows with a successful owner of a manufacturing company. If building such a business had been my goal back then, I would have probably seen the opportunity for what it was.

Think of this rule as putting on magical glasses that make potential resources that can help you reach your goal pop out from the background and move to the foreground of your attention. The more specific you are about your objective, the better your glasses will work.

Have a Vision

If you're reading this book, I assume you're no longer satisfied with the way the current is steering your life — or you want to learn how to steer it yourself even better. One of the most powerful tools that can help you identify what you want and inspire you to strive to get it is to create a vision for your life.

By writing down exactly what you want your average day to be like, what philosophies and core values will accompany you, with whom you'll be sharing your life, what you'll accomplish and what habits you'll cultivate, you'll design a personalized guide for your life.

EXERCISE #11: CREATE A VISION

I'll be the last person to say that you can "attract" things in life simply by thinking about them. Still, even though I don't believe in any magical powers, I strongly, *strongly* suggest creating a vision for your life.

Doing so is one of the best ways to gain clarity about how you want to shape your life. It will help you make better decisions that are aligned with the direction you want to pursue, as well as avoid going in the wrong direction (or worse, having no direction) in the first place.

How do you create a vision, then? It's not something that needs to follow a specific outline, but I'd generally suggest addressing the following parts of your life:

- Your perfect *average* day. What I mean by "average" is that you write about a regular day of yours, not your best day filled to the brim with excitement and life-changing events. Start by describing when you wake up, where, with whom (if anybody), and how you feel about the day ahead. Then proceed to describe your main activities for the day. It can be as long or as brief as you want — mine is just five sentences long.

- Describe your core philosophies and values. Again, be as detailed or vague as you want. I prefer to limit myself to my most important beliefs, so I mention how I manage my time (as the most precious resource in the world), how I look at the world (that it's abundant, that there's more than enough for everyone, and that I cultivate optimism), and what my most important driving forces are (freedom and independence to pursue growth and contribution).

- Describe relationships in your life. Include your spouse and children (if any), extended family if you want, friends, associates, and other key people in your life (mentors, employees, partners, colleagues, clients).

- Address your health and fitness. What's your diet like? How's your well-being? How often do you exercise and what do you look like?

Write your vision in the present tense, as in "I wake up together with my lovely spouse every day at five in the morning with a huge smile on my face, ready to work on our 7-figure manufacturing business."

Yes, it might sound a bit cheesy, but don't worry — nobody's going to read it but you.

Feel free to add whatever else you need to make this vision as real as possible. The goal is to identify what exactly you want to have in your life so that you have a guiding star.

I follow my vision with 10 personal rules I live by. I also have a document in which I note down goals I want to achieve, grouped as follows:

- The most important goal — limited to only one goal at a time, focused on the most life-changing objective.

- "Learn/try/experience" goals — things you want to experience just once (such as flying in a hot-air balloon or off-road driving); things you want to master (such as real estate investing), and things you want to learn, but not necessarily with an intention to dedicate your life to them (such as emergency first response or dancing salsa).

- Contribution goals — goals that extend beyond yourself and will make the world a better place. It can be running a small non-profit organization or even helping just one specific person.

- "Have/Finance/Business" goals — material things you'd like to have in your life. This includes business- or career- related goals.

- "Meet" goals — people you'd like to meet, just to shake hands or to befriend them.

- "Visit" goals — places you'd like to travel to.

Feel free to steal my structure and create a similar document that describes the goals you want to achieve.

YOU MUST IDENTIFY WHAT YOU WANT — AND GO AFTER IT: QUICK RECAP

1. You must identify what you want and go after it. Having a clear vision of your life will help you notice and take advantage of the right opportunities when they present themselves. Moreover, it all comes back to claiming control over your life. When you let the current steer you, you'll suffer from one of the greatest failures — the regret of not making the most out of the only stab at this thing called life we each have.

2. Create your own personal vision describing how you want your perfect life to be and make a list of goals you'd like to reach, in order to fine-tune the metaphorical glasses that help you recognize when an opportunity presents itself.

PART 3: A 5-Step Process to Cope With Failure and Bounce Back

I was excited to start working with Robert (name changed), a fitness coach who would finally help me build the chiseled physique I had wanted to reach for so many years. He set up a workout plan for me and told me how I should structure my diet. I had some reservations about his approach, but I ignored them and decided to go all in. After all, if you're hiring an expert to help you, you should trust his judgment.

Two months later I took pictures of myself, compared them to the pictures I took prior to working with Robert, and realized that nothing had changed. I had gained some weight, but my physique was the same — if not worse.

Soon, I started hating my workouts. To make the matters worse, Robert stopped replying to my emails or, if he replied after several days of silence, he only sent a vague response.

I was discouraged. No matter how hard I tried to follow the traditional bodybuilding advice, it always worked against me. Yet again, I had wasted time and energy on something that didn't deliver the promised results.

I was done with bodybuilding and I was done with stupid "bulking" diets that only made me gain fat. Because of the greatly increased calorie intake recommended by Robert, I got used to eating copious amounts of food and my weight crept up to alarming levels.

It took me three months to stabilize my eating habits and return to the weight I had had, prior to working with Robert. In the end, I lost almost six months going in circles.

I revised my goal, tweaked my strategy, optimized my lifestyle and today I'm not only much leaner, but also feel healthier, stronger, more flexible and positive about further improvements in my physique.

Failure can have a crushing effect if you take it personally. I hope that by now you no longer think of failure as a reason to give up. However, I know that it's hard to change your deeply-held beliefs overnight. Maybe you're already discouraged and have a hard time bouncing back and trying again.

In this part, I'll share with you the detailed step-by-step process of how to cope with failure. You'll learn how to process the failure and avoid a big mistake a lot of people make when they fail. Then you'll learn how to regain confidence, bounce back, and resume working on your goal.

This process addresses coping with failure for which you were at least partly to blame. If you couldn't do anything to prevent a negative event from happening, please refer to the chapter in which I give advice about dealing with a failure you couldn't prevent.

Please note that while some suggestions are based on scientific research, a lot of it is based primarily on my personal experience applied in my personal situation. As always, I invite you to be your own coach and choose what works best for you.

Chapter 14: Process the Failure

A soul-crushing failure *sucks*. It's disrespectful to trivialize anyone's failure by saying that they can simply "snap out of it." Right after a big failure, the last thing you want is somebody downplaying its significance in your life.

In some ways, failure is like coping with the loss of a loved one. Obviously, failure — no matter how crushing — can never match the suffering caused by losing a loved one, but the process of handling it shares some similarities with the process of dealing with grief.

The grieving process begins with denial, which is then followed by anger, bargaining (thinking about what you could have done to prevent the loss), depression, and acceptance.[39] These steps don't actually happen in a linear fashion, as people can alternate between these stages — feel depressed, then angry, then wish that things were different, and then get angry again.

When you fail, you probably go numb, deny it, and suppress the emotions caused by it. Then you wonder what you could have done to avoid the failure. Then you lose hope that you'll ever succeed, and ultimately, you accept what happened and move on.

The key to begin the process of bouncing back from failure is to accept that in the beginning of learning how to cope with it, you *will* feel numb and deny the negative emotions. Trying to suppress this stage will only prolong the process. If you can pull yourself together almost instantly, that's great. If not, don't rush it.

Let yourself feel the feelings that come with failure. Don't be tough on yourself. Let other people know you might not radiate with happiness for a period of time while you're trying to recover from your failure.

Each time my business failed, I went numb. I wondered how I could go on, now that yet another vehicle I thought would help me reach my goal was destroyed. In the beginning, this process took up to a couple of weeks, during which I'd be of little use to myself or anybody else.

I didn't know any better, so I was unable to bounce back quickly. Over time, I trained myself to become better at handling this stage. I'd deny the failure for a day or two, and then go into anger, which I would then channel into newly found resolve.

Eventually, I stopped denying the failure, reduced the amount of time spent on fruitless anger or depression, and learned to accept that it had happened. That's the good part about failing often: you get many opportunities to learn how to handle it, and you can quickly immunize yourself against it if you put in a conscious effort to do so.

When you get tired of feeling numb or in denial, you'll be ready to move on and continue the process of coping. This *always* happens sooner or later because humans *need* variety and it's impossible to stay in one emotional state forever. However, don't rush it. I know it's hard to feel hope, let alone even think about trying again, right after a failure, so give yourself the time necessary to move through all of the stages involved until you genuinely reach acceptance.

EMPOWERING STORY #7: ANNE WOJCICKI

Anne was a 23-year-old Yale graduate with a degree in biology when she got a job as a healthcare analyst on Wall Street.

To any typical 23-year-old, getting such a job would be a major success, but it wasn't for Anne, because she had been frustrated that such a wealthy country as the United States couldn't effectively provide even the most basic medical services to its citizens.

Anne became disillusioned with her Wall Street job when she attended an event, during which she heard insurers and accountants talking about how to "maximize the billing opportunity" when sick people sought care. That was when she realized that the system was never going to change from within.

As she commented during the SXSW festival, "Obesity is awesome from a Wall Street perspective. It's not just one disease — there are all sorts of related diseases to profit from."[40]

Several years into her lucrative career, she quit with the intention of enrolling in medical school. However, in the end, she decided to become a researcher.

Six years after quitting her Wall Street job, she channeled her disillusionment with the healthcare system into 23andMe, a privately held personal genomics and biotechnology company that she co-founded with Linda Avey and Paul Cusenza in 2006.

23andMe uses a simple saliva test to deliver ancestry reports and health-related components to consumers (at the time of writing this, the company offers health-related data to consumers in Canada and the United Kingdom and is working with the FDA to obtain regulatory approval to offer the same data in the US). It then uses this information for medical research to provide insight into why some people are more likely to get a disease than others and why people respond differently to disease treatment options and drugs.

Throughout the years, she met with adversity that came from all directions. The US Food and Drug Administration (FDA) ordered 23andMe to discontinue offering its service due to the lack of regulatory approval. In the tech and science world dominated by men, Anne still encounters scientists who (as she said in her interview for the *New York Times*) are like, "Oh honey, women aren't good at science."[41] In her personal life, Anne went through a difficult divorce.

Despite all of that, Anne and the 23andMe team is on track to help millions of people all over the world discover how their genetics can influence their risk for certain diseases, find out if they're a carrier for certain inherited conditions, and explore their genetic traits for everything from lactose intolerance to male pattern baldness. In addition to that, the acquired DNA information helps in researching some of the most common illnesses and disorders and, in the future, to develop drugs to treat them.

PROCESS THE FAILURE: QUICK RECAP

1. The first step to deal with a failure is to process it. Failure sucks, and it will sting. You'll probably feel resigned or frustrated. You might feel numb and hopeless. It's all normal, and you shouldn't deny these feelings.

2. Human beings need emotional variety. Sadness or discouragement after a failure will eventually convert into an opposite state, most likely anger. And that's when you'll proceed to the second or third phase discussed in the next chapters.

Chapter 15: Forgive Yourself

Some people feel self-hatred after a failure. They equate *failing* with *being a failure* as a human being. This leads them into a negative loop of self-criticism that makes them unable to constructively process a failure and bounce back. If you suffer from this problem, before you move on, you need to learn how to turn self-criticism into self-compassion.

According to scientific research, when you exhibit self-compassion after failing to meet your goals, you'll boost your mental resilience.[42] Self-kindness is also helpful in dealing with procrastination and enhances positivity.

Sounds good, but how do you actually stop criticizing yourself and become self-compassionate?

Here are a few ways to do so:

1. Imagine you're helping a friend cope with failure

Unless you're the world's worst friend, if your best friend failed at something, you'd encourage them instead of criticizing them, wouldn't you? It's incredible that we can lend kindness toward other people, but don't extend it toward ourselves.

EXERCISE #12: BE YOUR BEST FRIEND

It's hard to feel self-empathy when you're angry at yourself. It's easier to feel empathetic toward somebody else because then you're looking at the situation as a bystander, free of the negative emotions clouding your judgment. Why not look at yourself from that perspective, too?

Imagine that you're writing a letter to your best friend who happens to be an exact copy of you. What would you tell this person to help them overcome their feelings of inadequacy and self-hatred that arose from the failure? How would you convey the compassion you feel toward them? What would you write to remind this person that every person fails and that it doesn't mean they're inferior? How would you communicate that you understand the situation in which they found themselves and tell them that you care?

When you finish writing your letter, put it out of sight and forget about it. After a couple of days, read your letter and let the compassionate tones of the message sink into you. Upon reading the letter, you should feel more understanding and compassion toward yourself.

2. Reframe your critical self-talk

Your inner critic could be a great ally if its criticisms were constructive. Unfortunately, negative self-talk usually resembles something more like "you're a useless person" than "you didn't do it right because you were too distracted by those other tasks."

Why not turn your inner critic's criticisms into something useful? The first step is to become conscious of when your self-critical voice is present and how it talks to you. Then, as the person *observing* the critic instead of *being* the critic, you can hear the message, dissect it, and turn it into something more useful.

I know, it sounds a bit out-there, so let's dive into some more practical examples.

If you were on a diet and cheated because you were dealing with a painful problem and needed to comfort yourself, your self-critical voice might say something like: "You screwed up again. You had to mess everything up and comfort yourself with food. You're such a weak-willed loser!"

If you look for the underlying message, namely "you're an emotional eater," you can extract something useful from this self-criticism. But before doing so, you need to give yourself some compassion and acknowledge your challenges.

You *were* struggling and you needed some connection with yourself. Food has always worked for you as a source of comfort, so you decided to forgo your diet to improve your mood. There's no question that you *needed* to comfort yourself. Otherwise you wouldn't have been able to deal with the painful problem.

Now that you no longer feel guilty or at least accept why you did it, think about the negative consequences of your choice. Yes, you dealt with the problem, but it affected your diet, which directly affects your future health.

Could you find a way to connect with yourself that wouldn't involve eating? Could you try to connect with yourself by meditating, reading a book, going for a walk, listening to your favorite music, watching your favorite TV show, exercising, or doing any other thing that makes you feel good but isn't self-destructive? If it has to be eating, can it at least be eating something less caloric and healthier? If it can't, can you at least combine it with some exercise to reduce its negative effects on your well-being?

In addition to that, try looking at your inner critic's words from a different perspective.

If it says "You're lazy," you can admit that yes, sometimes you don't feel like doing things and that might pose a problem, but at the same time it's helpful because you only invest your time and energy into something you find worthwhile.

If it says "You can never focus on one thing at a time," you can agree that sometimes you *do* need to concentrate more, but at the same time your restlessness means you have a lot of energy and curiosity that you can use to help you achieve your goal.

Looking at self-criticism from a different, more empowering perspective will help you avoid thinking in terms of black and white. Your weaknesses might indeed cause problems, but they can also be helpful, so why hate yourself for them?

3. Nurture yourself

One of the documents I re-read from time to time to feel compassionate toward myself contains a list of ways I can go from a negative state (such as experiencing guilt or self-criticism) to making myself feel good. This simple list is a powerful ally in avoiding feeling guilt or anger at yourself when you fail.

Failure often leads to discouragement, which then turns into a strong need to comfort yourself. Pampering yourself when you feel bad will help you access a more positive state of mind, which will then help you overcome your self-critical voice. If you punish yourself with endless self-criticism, you'll only drive yourself deeper into the abyss of guilt. It will consequently take you even longer to bounce back.

Here are some suggestions on how to make yourself feel good:

- seek positive friends who can help you relax and offer reassurance;
- listen to music you love;
- meditate or engage in another type of meditative practice;
- practice a sport you love;
- go out for a walk;
- take a long, warm shower or bath;
- play with a pet;
- cuddle;
- have a massage.

A terrific resource with numerous practical exercises and guided meditations to become more self-compassionate is available at self-compassion researcher Dr. Kristin Neff's website www.self-compassion.org.

FORGIVE YOURSELF: QUICK RECAP

1. Some people who experience failure feel self-hatred, mistakenly equating the *act of failing* with *being a failure*. Learning how to turn self-criticism into self-compassion is crucial to cope with failure and bounce back with renewed confidence.

2. The three best ways to extend kindness toward yourself are to imagine you're helping a friend cope with failure (you can write a letter a best friend would write to you to help you lift your spirits); reframe your critical self-talk by looking for useful feedback when listening to your self-critical voice; or to nurture yourself by doing things that make you feel good.

Chapter 16: Change Your State

Don't fall victim to the self-help myth that when you're feeling down, you can snap out of it just like that by thinking happy thoughts. Well, maybe some people who've spent their entire lives learning how to control their emotions might be able to do that, but I can't — and I dare say, you probably can't, either.

The third step to overcome failure is to change your emotional state — to go from the negative feelings to a more positive mindset.

According to research performed by psychologist Daniel Wegner at the University of Virginia, if you're under stress (for example, right after a failure), trying to put yourself in a good mood by thinking happy thoughts can actually backfire.[43]

This happens because when you're under the mental load of a negative emotion, you don't have enough brainpower left to successfully distract yourself with positive thoughts. Try it yourself. It's easy to put yourself in a good mood if you aren't worried. Try the same while you're under stress, and you'll most likely fail.

It doesn't mean there's nothing you can do to stop feeling down or angry at the world, though. You can't snap out of it by merely thinking happy thoughts, but there are other ways to handle it.

The starting point is to lower your mental temperature, so to speak, to more manageable levels. If you're boiling with anger whenever you think about your failure, you aren't going to think about it coldly, analyze it, and bounce back from it — just like you can't have a healthy discussion with another person while you are shouting. You need to create some distance, cool off, and approach the situation again without anger boiling in your veins.

The self-nurturing activities we covered in the previous step are a good start toward changing your emotional state. The more immersive the activity is, the more effective it will be at taking your mind off the failure that is lingering in your head. Think about it as putting mental distance between you and the problem.

My two top strategies to access a more positive state of mind are rock climbing and going out for a walk with a friend.

When I climb, I need to dedicate my attention to the act of climbing. Since it's such a high-focus activity, it helps me forget about the failure, and when I come back home after a good workout, I usually have some good insights on how to deal with the situation.

Talking the failure over with your spouse or an empathetic friend is another winning strategy. I usually exercise at first to take off some initial steam, and I only turn to other people when I think more clearly.

Please note that you don't have to do it all yourself. If you get more energized when you spend time with people than by exercising, by all means change your state by surrounding yourself with people. This is highly personal, and you should discover your own methods of turning your unconstructive self into a person ready to bounce back.

The purpose of this step is to identify effective strategies — whether it's exercise, spending time alone, or reaching out to others — that will cool you down, help you look at the failure from a less emotionally-charged perspective, and open your mind to a possible new attempt.

EMPOWERING STORY #8: VERA WANG

In 1968, Vera Wang was a 19-years-old competitive figure skater who has been rigorously training since she was 8. Her dream was to make the US Olympics team. When she failed, she decided against pursuing competitive figure skating. Upon her graduation from college she began working for *Vogue*, a fashion magazine, as an assistant.

Her strong work ethic and dedication resulted in a quick promotion: just one year later she became the magazine's youngest-ever fashion editor. When she was turned down for the editor-in-chief position at *Vogue* after dedicating 15 years of her life to the magazine, she went on to work for Ralph Lauren as a design director. Having gained valuable experience and frustrated by a lack of stylish wedding dresses, she began her career as a bridal dress designer.

One might consider failing to make the Olympics team and being passed over for a promotion after 15 years of hard work a big failure. Yet for Vera, it was a blessing in disguise, as it motivated her to grow her career. Ultimately, it led her to becoming the world's most well-known bridal dress designer.

As Wang was quoted to say, "The ongoing, unmitigated truth is I would have done anything to be in fashion. I would have swept floors, which I did at *Vogue*, swept up hair from a model's haircut, pack up clothes, stay on a Friday night after the store closed to get it ready for the next day, which I did at Ralph (Lauren). Still, I always felt privileged to have this job. How lucky am I to have gotten here?"[44]

When asked if she ever thought she'd become so successful, she replied: "I never thought I'd be successful. It seems in my own mind that in everything I've undertaken, I've never quite made the mark. But I've always been able to put disappointments aside. Success isn't about the end result, it's about what you learn along the way."[45]

CHANGE YOUR STATE: QUICK RECAP

1. The third step is to change your emotional state. If you've dealt with the first and second phase of handling a failure, now you're probably angry that you failed or you alternate between feeling sad and pissed. Neither state is useful if you want to process the failure, because they cloud your judgment with strong emotions that make you unable to look at the failure from a more neutral point of view.

2. Engage in activities that will help you let off some steam and take your mind off the failure. Staying home and fuming at the failure isn't going to change anything; you need to put some distance between yourself and the failure to be able to learn from it and bounce back.

Chapter 17: Learn From It

This step is as simple as it sounds: identify what you can learn from the failure. This will help you look at the failure in terms of useful real-world feedback, rather than a painful blow without any benefits.

I usually search for one key lesson that can make the biggest difference in my future endeavors, but it's a good idea to identify several potential causes for your failure and then try to find a common link between them.

For example, my failure to reduce my body fat level to below 10% was caused by several factors. I could have eaten more vegetables to feel fuller. I could have avoided occasional naps during the day which always made me hungry. I could have eaten more salads and less rice. I could have maintained a smaller, more sustainable caloric deficit.

But in the end, it wasn't about those little details. The overarching problem was deeper than that: my motivation wasn't strong enough. I thought it was, but it didn't address an important part of my life that would offer a powerful boost of motivation — namely, the fact that reducing my body fat would greatly improve my climbing performance. When I restarted my diet with this strong motivation in mind, suddenly everything fell into place.

Please note that it might take time to figure out the key lesson from your failure. I don't expect you to know it instantly; after all, if you had known it beforehand, you wouldn't have failed. If you're struggling to find the answer, seek outside help: ask your friends or family, or join an online forum and ask people who have dealt with the same problem.

This step is essential because it will help you avoid making the same mistake in the future. When you pinpoint the most probable cause of your failure, you will see your failure in a new way, providing hope for the future. After all, you've just discarded an approach that doesn't work, so now you'll be more likely to succeed, just like you're more likely to pick the correct answer if you go from four possible answers to three.

LEARN FROM IT: QUICK RECAP

1. Create a list of lessons you've learned from your failure. Then, try to find a common thread — one key lesson that will help you change your approach and succeed with the next attempt.

2. Take your time to identify the key lesson from the failure. It's better to spend a few days more analyzing your failure than to resume working on your goal, only to fail yet again due to the same (unidentified) cause. This step is essential to leverage failure as a valuable tool for your future endeavors.

Chapter 18: Restart Your Efforts

When you've gone through the entire process and feel ready to resume working on your goal, it's time to restart your efforts. Considering that the entire process might take weeks before you reach this step, be prepared to face some initial reluctance upon realizing that you're back where you started. This feeling should pass once you have some first tiny wins.

There are two ways to resume working on your goal. Both can be equally effective, so experiment with both.

1. You jump back into things with a big bang

Often when I fail, I feel as if I had lost all momentum. This is a depressing thought because I'm an impatient person by nature and want to achieve my goals as quickly as possible. That's why I usually focus on generating some visible results as quickly as possible so that I can almost immediately feel that I'm back on track.

I used to wake up past noon and stay up until early morning hours. I wanted to change my routine and become an early riser. It took me several attempts to reach this goal.

At first, I would set my alarm clock for 10 a.m. and then (over the next couple of weeks) each day I would change the alarm to wake me up 5 or 10 minutes earlier. Soon, I would find myself unable to get up that early and start waking up past noon again. Then I would bounce back, set the alarm clock for 10 a.m. and try again. This approach didn't work well because I didn't feel there was such a big difference between waking up at 10 a.m. and waking up around noon.

When I set my alarm for 5 a.m., I finally had a breakthrough. Waking up so early was more exciting, and it gave me a powerful sense of getting instant results — which, in this case, I was able to maintain in the long term.

2. You start slowly and get yourself back in the groove

Sometimes it might be better to bounce back slowly, by getting yourself back in the groove with tiny steps. One possible application of this approach is when you want to resume your exercise regimen. Of course, you can restart your routine with a hard workout, but the most probable result will be subsequent muscle soreness that will make it harder to keep going. Unless you don't mind the pain, a better approach might be to start with a brief, easy session, and then slowly make your workouts longer and harder.

I once had a longer break from writing new books. To get myself back in the groove, I slowly eased myself into things by brainstorming potential topics and organizing my thoughts. Then, the next day, I created a general outline. Then I created a detailed book outline, started writing the easiest chapter, and took it from there.

Taking an extreme approach by writing several thousand words on the first day would have made it more difficult to resume writing, as I generally find that my creativity "muscle" needs to be warmed up slowly over a couple of days.

BOUNCE BACK: QUICK RECAP

1. The last step in recovering from failure is to restart your efforts. It's possible you'll feel some initial reluctance upon realizing that you're back where you started, but it should quickly pass once you first have some tiny wins.

2. You can choose from two approaches: start with a big bang and generate quick, visible results with an extreme approach, or take tiny steps to slowly ease yourself back into a routine. Both approaches can be equally effective; pick whichever you feel works best for your situation.

PART 4:
Three Master Strategies to Build Strength to Keep Going

The burn quickly crept from my legs into my arms and rapidly flooded my upper body. I gasped for air, reminding myself over and over again that I would finish the lap soon and the pain would go away.

When I finished the lap and my breathing had stabilized a little, my coach had great news for me: I was about to perform another set of shadow-boxing for four minutes and then run another lap as quickly as I could.

When I finished the second lap (which was even more excruciating that the first one), — there was still one more round of shadow-boxing and then yet another lap of sprinting. I'm pretty sure it didn't actually look like sprinting, but more like running in slow motion.

It would be so easy to slow down, act as if I was giving it my best while keeping a relatively comfortable pace. My coach wouldn't know. But I knew that I had to find strength in myself to keep going as quickly as possible, because that's the purpose of training — even if at the very moment you absolutely hate it and feel as if you're about to faint or throw up.

It doesn't matter if you're training sprints, fighting against immense pain during physical rehabilitation, or feel discouraged in the face of yet another insurmountable obstacle. You build strength to keep going when you face adversity and do it anyway.

However, how do you build such determination, and how do you keep it in the long term? That's what we're going to talk about in this part. Instead of giving you a long list of little tips that each make a small difference, we'll focus on three master strategies that deliver big results. When you implement them together, you'll benefit from a powerful synergistic effect.

Chapter 19: Develop a Passion

The best way to build long-term resolve is to develop a long-term passion that consistently motivates you to persist in spite of challenges. When performed over the long term, it will build up your reserves of mental strength while you're enjoying yourself.

Being able to draw parallels between this activity and your other goals will prove to be one of the greatest assets you'll be able to access to keep going. Think of it as an exercise in building a thicker skin and gaining valuable experiences that you can leverage when you face adversity while working on other goals.

I could easily draw numerous parallels between rock climbing and goal achievement — and I frequently do, to help me achieve my goals. Such an all-encompassing approach to developing determination will deliver the best results. You'll learn from your own experience instead of learning from a book, and all of that will happen as a side effect of your passion.

After facing so many stressful and uncomfortable situations on a cliff or on an indoor climbing wall, I'm now better equipped to find strength to keep going when faced with other negative circumstances. I can recall a difficult situation when climbing and translate it to the situation I'm facing right now — and remind myself that I can push through it.

In climbing, you often try the same route over and over again for weeks or months, always falling at the same difficult point. Then, eventually one day you succeed and progress further. Mere words can't describe the elation you have when you realize that your determination has finally paid off — and the best part is that this experience helps you apply the same level of dedication to other parts of your life, too.

Sometimes you climb a route that is within your abilities, but your negative self-talk prevents you from climbing it successfully. Oftentimes, it's not about your physical performance, but your mental attitude. I once spent 20 minutes hanging on a cliff, repeatedly trying and falling on the same move, over and over again. Despite telling myself numerous times that there was no way I would be able to perform it, I finally succeeded and realized that I had been limiting my performance myself with my useless negative talk.

Such experiences build new neural pathways that transform you into a new person. In my case, climbing turned me into a more determined person. I now know — and experienced it firsthand over and over again — that with enough attempts, and despite self-doubt, I can reach my goals.

I can't overstate the importance of having such experiences yourself. It's one thing to read about them in a book; it's a completely different thing when you experience them yourself and draw your own conclusions. Don't just gloss over these paragraphs. This is one of the most important lessons I can share with you when it comes to building a successful life. You *need* to learn through your own experiences.

EXERCISE #13: DEVOTE YOURSELF

Find an activity that you can be passionate about over the long term. It needs to put you in situations in which you can grow your mental toughness. Ideas include: all kinds of sports, public speaking, standup comedy, dancing, yoga, traveling. Ideally, your passion should require you to step outside your comfort zone on a regular basis, although writing, programming, cooking or artistic skills such as illustration, painting or photography can also serve as valuable teachers.

Here are some pointers to help you find the right activity for you:

1. You can easily engage in it on a regular basis. For example, surfing would not be a good choice if it takes you five hours to reach the coast.

2. It's something that engages you physically and mentally so that you can experience the state of *flow*, a state of being fully immersed in the activity.

3. You must be able to learn life lessons from this activity and apply them to other activities.

4. You must believe that if you persist at it, you will get better at it. You won't stick to anything in the long term if you doubt your abilities to improve.

5. Tony Robbins defines addiction as a behavior (negative or positive) that meets at least three of six human needs: certainty, variety, significance, connection/love, growth and contribution. Your activity must also meet three of those same needs. For example, if something you do makes you feel safe (meets the need for certainty), important (meets the need for significance) and loved (meets the need for connection/love), you'll engage in it on a regular, permanent basis.

It's important to note that you probably won't like this activity all the time. For example, as much as I love rock climbing, whenever I climb a hard route, I often feel like I want to stop and be safe and sound back on the ground. However, the moment I'm back on the ground —

or haven't been climbing for a couple of days — I feel the need to do it again. That's a great example of something I'm devoted to, even though it's often so challenging I want to stop.

Reading books won't be a good candidate for this particular use because it isn't super challenging (unless you want to read the world's most boring book), and neither will watching TV series. You must see this activity as a vehicle for rapid and significant personal growth.

If you already have such an activity in your life, good for you! Think of at least five difficult situations you faced when performing this activity and how you overcame them. Even something as mundane as hitting the golf ball in a completely wrong direction, but then still winning the game thanks to persistence, can become a great metaphor to help you reach other goals.

In addition to learning valuable lessons you can apply to other goals, a long-term passion teaches you good old work ethics and determination.

Nowadays, few people are able to dedicate themselves to something over the long term. Commitments and promises are no longer seen as sacrosanct. People love the rush of trying one new thing after another without ever becoming well-familiarized with something.

When you devote yourself to a certain activity and it becomes a long-term passion, you'll stick to it no matter what happens. It will be too hard to break the habit just because you no longer feel like doing it. Such a devotion to a passion is a powerful master strategy to encourage positive mindset changes, build grit, and grow you as a person. I consider it a must-have for people who want to achieve their full potential.

EMPOWERING STORY #9: ELLIE ROBINSON

Ellie Robinson was born with a form of dwarfism that impairs movement. Despite her condition, she started swimming at the age of four. In 2012, when she was 11, her parents took her to the 2012 London Paralympics to watch Ellie Simmonds, the four-time gold medalist in swimming who suffers from the same condition.

Inspired by Simmonds, Ellie decided to start competing. Unfortunately, due to another condition of hers (Perthes' disease, which disrupts blood flow to the hip and causes immense pain), she had to stop training for six months. Belinda Smith, her first coach at Northampton Swimming Club said about Ellie's resolve, "Even when she came back in about June 2013, she couldn't dive, she couldn't turn and she had to be helped into the water."[46]

In spite of her condition and a forced training break, she made quick progress and qualified for a spot on Great Britain's Paralympics team in Rio de Janeiro 2016 — with a time better than her idol Ellie Simmonds in the 50m butterfly. At the 2016 Paralympics in Rio de Janeiro, she won the gold medal and set a new record time in the women's S6 50m butterfly.

Despite requiring daily physiotherapy, she trains five days a week for a total of 15 hours and is in the pool at 5 a.m. on two mornings a week.

When asked about her personal statement, she said: "One of the main quotes I like to remind myself is 'don't let your fear of what could happen make nothing happen,' so I can make the most of my opportunities."[47]

DEVELOP A PASSION: QUICK RECAP

1. Developing a passion that forces you to step outside your comfort zone and/or delivers other lessons that you can apply when working on other goals is a powerful master strategy for becoming a successful person. It's one thing to read about someone's experiences and quite another to draw parallels between your own experiences; nothing can replace the latter in its effectiveness and applicability to your own situation.

2. When you devote yourself to a passion over the long term, you'll also learn how to be more determined and maintain a strong work ethic — two traits many people sorely lack in today's world of instant gratification.

Chapter 20: Adopt the Experimental Approach

Whenever you set high expectations and assume you can't lose, you set yourself up for a potential knock-out-like blow of discouragement. When you repeat this behavior frequently, you will rapidly deplete your resources of willpower.

I frequently hear entrepreneurs saying things like: "Even if I only convert 1% of visitors to my website — and this is unlikely, as I'll surely convert 2% or 3% — I'd still make a lot of money." They forget that there are numbers lower than 1%, and their conversion rate might be 0.3%, 0.05%, or even 0%. When they don't reach their goal, they feel bitter and angry. After all, even in the most pessimistic scenario they should have been rolling in it now.

In the opening words of this book, I talked about my failures from investing in video courses. Despite losing a lot of money, I mentioned that I didn't feel angry or particularly disappointed. I protected myself against those emotions because I used a certain strategy that we're going to talk about now.

While it's good to have high hopes and set big goals, this applies primarily to objectives you're already knowledgeable about, as you can more or less accurately calculate your odds. However, even then, you should still account for the fact that failure is always a possibility and nobody has an innate golden touch.

For this reason, if you aren't entirely sure about a certain goal of yours, it makes sense to approach it as an experiment.

I set aside a portion of my monthly business budget to run new experiments. Instead of expecting loads of money coming my way from every single new endeavor, I consider the money I invest in a new idea as money spent to learn. I don't expect a fast return (if any). If I make a return, great. If not, it was an experiment anyway, and there's nothing to be angry about.

Such an approach doesn't mean I don't try my best to make it work; it's just a mind hack that helps me overcome fear of failure and reduce performance anxiety. It's crucial to instill in your mind that the money (or other resources you use) is *lost* from the start of the experiment. You can use the word "invested" instead of "lost," but don't fool yourself — if it's an experiment, prepare yourself to lose it all.

This simple tweak in your attitude will prevent you from procrastinating out of fear or becoming discouraged when you fail. After all, it was an *experiment*, without a guaranteed positive outcome.

Note that this strategy can increase your chances of success because, if you consider your new undertaking an experiment, you'll be more willing to approach it as a scientist, tweak your approach, change certain variables, and find a winning mix.

In business, setting aside a part of your budget for experiments will make you more likely to innovate and achieve unexpected big wins. He or she who sows more, reaps more.

This master strategy isn't limited only to business, though. In sports, ego often plays a key role. You don't want to lose or perform badly, so you avoid uncertain and difficult things.

In rock climbing, I often convince myself to approach routes I feel apprehensive about by telling myself it's just an experiment. When I don't expect to climb a difficult route, I can forget about bad performance and simply focus on performing my experiment — and whether it ends during my next move or at the top of the route is irrelevant. What matters is that I tried something new.

I used to tell myself the same thing when fighting against my shyness. I would approach a female stranger, telling myself it was just an experiment. I could only gain from the experience. Since I wasn't expecting a "return on my investment," I could approach her with little to no fear: it didn't matter if I was rejected or not. The experiment ran its course regardless of what happened, just like scientists don't stop an experiment because they don't like its results.

Adopting the experimental approach is crucial for long-term goals because they take numerous attempts to achieve. You most likely won't succeed with your first business idea, and chances are you won't succeed with the second one, either. If you approach both attempts as experiments, you'd be more likely to keep going than if you assumed right away that your first idea would make you a millionaire.

Again, it's good to have positive expectations, but for the purpose of maintaining long-term determination, it makes sense to treat your efforts as experiments. They may deliver the results you're after, but if not, they can help you discard the wrong approach without feeling like you failed.

Change Doesn't Have to Be Permanent

Successful entrepreneur Noah Kagan points out in his interview with popular blogger Tynan that change doesn't have to be permanent,[48] It's hard to make daunting changes if you believe you can't back out of them.

Think of your big decision as an experiment that you can conclude at any moment, and it will cease to be daunting or impossible to revert.

If you want to switch to a plant-based diet, the thought that you'll *never* be able to eat meat, fish, or eggs again makes it pretty much impossible for most people to take such a decision. How about going on a plant-based diet for only a month or just a week and seeing how you feel?

If you want to start your career as a freelancer, you don't have to give in your notice at your job and go for broke. How about applying for a couple of small gigs and working on the weekends to test the waters?

Don't overthink it. Find a way to introduce a big change in your life with little commitment and investment on your part. If it works well, make it a permanent change. If you don't like it, stop doing it. There's little you can lose, and a lot you can potentially gain.

You're in control of how much of a risk you want to take with your decisions. You can dip your toes in the water and invest as little as possible, or you can place a larger bet that will result in a bigger win or a more painful loss.

When I started out with my self-publishing business, I ran small experiments. I decided to spend $50 instead of $10 to design a cover or risk $50 to test a new promotional service. Note that safe experiments don't always come with limited upside. Spending just $40 more on a professional book cover comes with little risk, while it can potentially dramatically increase sales.

Later on, when I had more money and my "risk muscle" became stronger, I started running bigger experiments. Recently I spent several thousand dollars on hiring a business consultant. In the end, I realized that the solutions offered to me by the consultant weren't right for me in the long term.

I decided to cut my losses, which meant losing the money I'd already invested in hiring the consultant, as well as refunding money to people who had pre-ordered the product I had started working on.

Prior to starting this experiment, I knew that the potential upside was big, but I was also fine with the fact that if it did not work out, I'd lose a lot of money. In the end, the experiment was still worth it, as it helped me clarify the long-term direction of my business.

People often give up on their goals, not because their experiments fail, but because they don't run them at all and consequently, don't evolve.

If it weren't for my numerous experiments in my self-publishing business, I wouldn't have become a bestselling self-published author.

My losses amount to thousands of dollars and hundreds of hours of my time, but my wins are a healthy multiple bigger.

Embrace experiments, and even if most of them fail, you only need one or two to score big wins.

EXERCISE #14: DEVISE AN EXPERIMENT

Is there anything that could help you achieve your goal, but you're afraid of doing it because you fear you'll lose money or time or get discouraged if it were not to work out?

Approach it as an experiment. Run it with the sole intention of gathering data for a short period of time so that it isn't overwhelming. If you don't have a good tolerance for risk, start as small as you can and gently exercise your risk muscle along the way.

Set a budget: it can be in monetary terms ($500 to test a new marketing channel), time (4 weeks of following a new diet), quantity (write 20,000 words to see if you can write a short story and become a professional writer), and get started.

Your goal is to run the experiment until you gather enough data to draw good conclusions. Consider the experiment successful as long as you gain useful information from it.

ADOPT THE EXPERIMENTAL APPROACH: QUICK RECAP

1. Setting high expectations and never taking into account the fact that you can lose can lead to discouragement if you fail. The solution is to adopt the experimental mindset, in which you consider a new undertaking an experiment. Your goal ceases to be about achieving success; it's about testing your hypothesis.

2. To conduct a successful experiment, set a budget (choose a specific amount of resources you'll dedicate to it, be it money, time or energy) and run it until you get solid data.

It's important to approach it as a short-term experiment. Even if you'd like to introduce a new change permanently, it's a good idea to run it as an experiment first for a limited period of time. This will transform the daunting big decision into a less overwhelming little experiment.

Chapter 21: Find Value Regardless of Results

Often the chief reason why it's so hard to keep going is when you feel that what you're doing is useless. It's understandable that you get frustrated when you get no results. Who would want to continue doing something that is worthless?

This reasoning in itself makes sense, but your efforts are rarely really worthless. Even if it seems like you aren't making any progress at all, there's almost always some value in what you're doing. Identifying it can help you push forward.

It's best to explain this master strategy with some real-world examples.

Over the years, I launched numerous businesses. Most of them were utter failures. Even in my otherwise successful self-publishing business, I had numerous flops. Sales of some of my products barely covered the expenses to produce them, and I never got compensated for the time I had invested in creating them. I also had high hopes for some books that never took off or spent money translating my book into another language, only to see a couple of sales.

Aside from adopting the experimental mindset, what helped me keep going was realizing that despite not reaching the results I was after, I still had helped somebody. I still created something of value, so my efforts had a meaning.

If I were convinced there were no value whatsoever in my business undertakings, I'd definitely have a harder time finding the motivation to keep going and trying new things. Who wants to take actions that have no impact?

When I failed over and over again with my efforts to achieve a chiseled physique, I could have said it was all worthless. I wasted weeks following a diet only to realize that nothing had changed in my appearance. However, even if nothing changed in my body, I could still find *some* value in my attempt. I learned something new about dieting. I had the opportunity to exercise my willpower. I discarded an ineffective approach to dieting.

In climbing, I often climb the same route over and over again and find myself unable to progress further. I stop at the exact same moment, and a bystander could say that my attempts are worthless because there's no progress, but there's always some value in each attempt.

Maybe I'll climb the easier portion of the route more fluidly. Maybe repeated attempts will improve my conditioning and in a few months, I'll be able to push forward. And even if none of those things happened, the activity itself is still of value: I get to do something I love, exercise my body, and spend time with friends.

I once spent several weeks taking Arabic classes to prepare myself for a trip to Oman, a beautiful Arabic-speaking country in the Persian Gulf region. I wanted to be able to hold some basic conversations in the language and read at least some of the most common signs you see in every city.

Aside from the fact that my goal was too ambitious and I failed to prepare myself properly, it was a big waste of time because pretty much nobody wanted to use Arabic with me, nor were they impressed by my lackluster skills. Because of a huge number of immigrants from India, Pakistan, and Bangladesh who are living in Oman, pretty much every single interaction you have on a daily basis is with a person who doesn't speak Arabic (or good English, for that matter). Omanis are forced to use English with pretty much everybody, and since their skills are so good, they don't expect anybody to speak Arabic to them nor do they care if somebody does speak it.

It was a worthless undertaking to learn Arabic, wasn't it? I should have been angry and discouraged because I had lost money and time and didn't get to use the skill I had spent them on.

It wasn't really a waste. Despite my failure and few opportunities to use what I had learned, I could still use it on some limited occasions. I still learned a little about another language and my mind opened to a new way of thinking. I'll continue my practice of learning the most basic language skills whenever I travel to a country whose language I don't speak, because I still find it gratifying.

In relationships, a person can spend weeks or months trying to save a relationship. In the end, their attempts can be for naught, as the relationship terminates anyway.

It would be easy to say that their attempts were worthless. They only wasted their time trying to save something that couldn't have been saved. Perhaps so, but at the same time, they got to at least try. They fought for the relationship, they invested their time and energy, and they did *something* — and this something in itself is often of enough value that, even if it doesn't change the outcome, it was worth it. As they say, it's better to regret something you've done than something you haven't.

EXERCISE #15: DIG FOR VALUE

Think of three projects of yours that you think were an utter waste of resources. Maybe you started a side business and you lost a considerable amount of money. Maybe you spent a few months learning French but then nobody in Paris tolerated your attempts to speak their language. Or perhaps you came up with a project that you presented to your boss but they turned it down, even though it was a great idea.

Now, come up with at least five reasons why there was some value in your attempts, even if it seems they were worthless.

Your business failed, but you learned something new about entrepreneurship. You didn't get to use French with Parisians, but you can still speak a foreign language and might get a better job in the future, thanks to this skill. Your project wasn't approved by your boss, but there's probably a record somewhere that you took the initiative — and you still got to do something and learn something new.

Performing this exercise regularly for any failed activity will help you avoid discouragement that comes from the erroneous assumption that you wasted your resources. Remember: as long as you're not literally flushing money down the drain, there's always some value in what you're doing, even if it's hard to notice it.

FIND VALUE REGARDLESS OF RESULTS: QUICK RECAP

1. When you consider your efforts a complete waste of time, you'll undoubtedly feel discouraged and not want to keep going. Nobody wants to waste their time or energy on things that produce no results. That's why it's so important to find reasons why your undertakings — even if you consider them a big failure and an utter waste of resources — were valuable.

2. Whenever you catch yourself thinking that something was a complete waste, try to identify something of value that you gained, thanks to this experience. Perhaps your business didn't succeed, but you still helped a few clients. Maybe you couldn't stick to your diet, but now you have a better understanding of proper nutrition. Perhaps somebody else was chosen for the position you applied for, but you still made a good impression that can help you land a job in the future.

PART 5: Four Reasons to Give Up

When I first learned that you can make money selling stock options with a mathematic approach, I was excited. I'd been looking for an investment strategy that wouldn't rely on luck or incredible analytical skills.

I soon hit the first obstacle: no matter how hard I tried, I couldn't understand slightly more advanced concepts. I figured that if I opened a demo account and tested the strategies with virtual money, perhaps I would learn how it works in actual practice. I was dumbfounded when (according to all of my calculations) I should have made money, but instead I lost it.

I went back to studying theory, determined to understand every single part of the process. I reached out to other investors and asked them questions, referred to videos, articles, and books, but I still couldn't figure it out. It was as if somebody sent me back in time to Ancient Greece — I couldn't make sense of this world and its language.

In the end, despite my initial enthusiasm and persistence, I gave up. I'm glad I did so, because I avoided losing a lot of money. I also discovered that I have a penchant for simplicity in investing, and selling stock options is anything but simple. In the end, this experience helped me choose an approach that was better suited for my personality.

So far, we have covered how to deal with various types of failure, recover from them, and resume working on your goals. However, it doesn't always make sense to be persistent. Sometimes failure signals that you should stop because you're wasting your time.

In the last part of the book you'll learn about the four most common reasons to give up. After you finish reading this part, you should have a clear understanding of when to continue with your objective or move on.

Chapter 22: Give Up If It Isn't Congruent With You

Among the most famous Instagram celebrities, 19-year old Australian model Essena O'Neill had it all: more than 600,000 followers; around 2,000 uploaded photos, in which she showed off her fit body wearing designer dresses in beautiful locations; and it didn't hurt that she was making $2000 per promotional post.

Yet one day she quit her lucrative business. As she said in a deleted vlog commenting on her decision, "I, myself, was consumed by it. This was the reason why I quit social media: for me, personally, it consumed me. I wasn't living in a 3D world."

Some goals or achievements — as exciting as they can be — can turn your life into a nightmare. Instagram models like Essena pay a high price for their success. Each day, she had to spend hours trying to take a perfect picture, hide her every flaw, and pretend she was living in a fantasy world.

We live in an era where unrealistic standards are forced upon us at every corner. We're to follow them at all cost, even at the expense of our self-worth or happiness.

After all, if you don't post your travel pictures on Facebook, it's as if you didn't travel at all. If you don't share a picture of your meal on Instagram, you didn't go to this new fancy restaurant. If you don't post hundreds of pictures hanging out with your friends, you don't have friends.

This problem isn't limited to social media only. People waste years of their lives in constant stress, chasing goals they themselves would never pursue if it weren't for their social conditioning or the admiration they can get.

Society pressures young people to go to the college. And those who want to consider an alternative career choice or start a business? Nah, too risky. It's better to study, get your degree and put your faith in your employer who can (and unfortunately, at some point probably will) fire you overnight.

There's this widespread belief that you need to find a life partner, have kids, settle down, get a mortgage, waste your life in traffic jams and retire to enjoy your golden years (if you can afford it). It's the American dream, baby. What about those who don't want to start a family, who don't want to drown in debt, or who have dreams of traveling the world or doing something other than following the conventional path? Better adapt yourself to the "real world" and be like everyone else.

Then there are millions of people all over the world who go to a job that (even if it's lucrative and makes them a respected member of society) is living hell for them. But since the common idea of success is making as much money as you can, at the expense of your health and time, they keep on living in silent suffering rather than consider the *preposterous* idea that maybe they should find an alternative path that would allow them to enjoy their lives.

I guess you can tell that "undisputed" social mores make my blood boil. I don't want you to waste your life chasing things that don't matter to you because you were fooled by a social dogma that you *should* chase them. This is the first common reason why you should give up on certain goals: if you're chasing them not for yourself, but out of the need to conform.

I went to college because my parents wanted me to do so. According to them (and the great majority of society), you need to go to college if you want to succeed in life.

It doesn't matter that most professors base their knowledge on handbooks released in the last century and won't teach you anything even remotely useful in the real world.

I studied business administration from people who have never run a business. Most of them have never worked outside of academia. I forced myself to exist in this ridiculous reality that few people question, for the sake of accomplishing the "crucial" goal of acquiring a formal education.

I put an end to this suffering within less than two years. Attending college was one of the unhappiest periods of my life. The only regret I have is that I didn't drop out sooner. At least I got to experience firsthand how ridiculous the system is.

Revise your goals and ask yourself if you're chasing something *you* really want or if it's something you're pursuing because somebody else has established that it's a worthwhile goal.

You Want It, But It Costs You Too Much

You may find yourself in a situation in which you're chasing a goal you *do* want to achieve, but it generates too much daily suffering. It's impossible to reach your goals without some level of pain and discomfort, but if it costs you too much, it's probably not worth it.

I once owned a company that sold software to real estate agents. Few things are worse to me than trying to sell strangers my product over the phone, yet that's precisely what I had to do in this business, on a daily basis. Even though there was a lot of potential in the idea, I sold this company because its effect on my stress levels was overwhelming. It wasn't worth it to sacrifice my mental health to reach the goal of turning this business into the best solution provider in the industry.

If a goal you're working on makes you stressed out no end, ruins your health, destroys your relationships, or negatively affects your self-worth so much that you're starting to hate yourself, give up. Don't fool yourself that it will go away. Yes, you can push yourself and keep going, but at what cost? It's only a matter of time before you give up anyway, due to all the pent-up rage boiling inside you, or the stress will ruin your health and you'll *have* to give up.

However, let's be clear: sometimes you don't have a choice and you need to do something unenjoyable. All goals come with some inconveniences. I heavily dislike certain parts of self-publishing, but I don't deal with those aspects on a regular basis. If I hated writing, how long do you think I'd be able to persevere, if my main job is to write thousands of words each month?

As long as it's a rare occurrence, it won't affect your long-term performance. If you feel negative emotions on a daily basis, the process isn't sustainable and you likely won't be able to sustain it long enough to reach your goal. Some people are more skilled at tolerating the things they hate in the long-term, but even they will eventually pay the price — in lost energy, bad health, damaged relationships or other negative consequences of living a lifestyle that is incongruent with your personality.

Procrastination often signals that you should give up. Whenever I procrastinate about something, I know that deep down I don't care about it as much as I think I do. If I did, I wouldn't constantly put it off. This makes me rethink the importance of a given goal.

If you find yourself in the same situation and you usually don't procrastinate with other tasks, perhaps you're trying to stay faithful to a goal that you should give up.

EMPOWERING STORY #10: TONI MORRISON

It was 1933. Toni Morrison was two when her parents fell behind with their monthly $4 rent. Because of their inability to pay, the landlord set fire to the house while the family was inside. Toni was too young to remember the event, but she remembered her parents telling her about it and the important lessons about resilience they passed on to her.

In 1993, she recounted the event in an interview for the *Washington Post*: "It was this hysterical, out-of-the-ordinary, bizarre form of evil. If you internalized it, you'd be truly and thoroughly depressed because that's how much your life meant. For $4 a month somebody would just burn you to a crisp. So what you did instead was laugh at him, at the absurdity, at the monumental crudeness of it. That way you gave back yourself to yourself. You know what I mean? You distanced yourself from the implications of the act. That's what laughter does. You take it back. You take your life back. You take your integrity back."[49]

Living in a period of racial segregation, she would deal with adversity on a frequent basis. When she first encountered lunch counters she could not sit at, stores that wouldn't accept her money and buses where she couldn't sit at the front, she used the same lesson her parents taught her. As she said in an interview for the *New York Times* in 2015, "I think it's a theatrical thing. I always felt that everything else was the theater. They didn't really mean that. How could they? It was too stupid."[50]

Despite living in the times when black people were denigrated, Toni would never let it affect her self-worth. As she said in a 1994 interview for *New York Times*, "Interestingly, I've always felt deserving. Growing up in Lorain, my parents made all of us feel as though there were these rather extraordinary deserving people within us. I felt like an aristocrat — or what I think an aristocrat is. I always knew we were very poor. But that was never degrading. I remember a very important lesson that my father gave me when I was 12 or 13. He said, 'You know, today I welded a perfect seam and I signed my name to it.' And I said, 'But, Daddy, no one's going to see it!' And he said, 'Yeah, but I know it's there.' So when I was working in kitchens, I did good work."[51]

After completing college and graduate school, she married and had a son. While she was months into her second pregnancy, her marriage fell apart and Toni became a single mother with two sons. Brave and strong in spite of the hardships, she moved 400 miles away (with her children) when she received a job as an editor with L. W. Singer, a textbook division of Random House that was based in Syracuse, NY. Two years later she transferred to Random House in New York City and became the first black woman senior editor in the fiction department in the history of the company.

In the meantime, she spent five years working on her first story. As a single mother doing all she could to support her two children, her time for writing was limited. She woke up at 4 a.m. to write. As she said in the *New Yorker* interview in 2003, "I stole time to write. Writing was my other job—I always kept it over there, away from my 'real' work as an editor or teacher."[52] After her early morning writing sessions she went to work where, as an editor of black literature, she was instrumental in fostering a new generation of African American authors.

Her first book, *The Bluest Eye*, took five years to finish. It didn't sell well until it was put on the reading lists of black-studies departments of several colleges. It would take 17 years more before Toni Morrison would release her most successful novel, *Beloved*. Despite critical acclaim and international renown, it wasn't until a group of 48 black critics and writers protested the lack of national recognition of Morrison's works that she would get recognized for her contribution to American literature.

In 1988, at the age of 57 and more than 23 years after she began working on her first book, Toni Morrison won the Pulitzer Prize for fiction. Five years later, in 1993, she was awarded the Nobel Prize in Literature — the first black woman of any nationality to win the prize. In 2012, she was honored with the Presidential Medal of Freedom.

Perhaps the best words describing her mental resilience and unbending will in the face of adversity come from her 2012 novel *Home*, in which she writes: "Look to yourself. You free. Nothing and nobody is obliged to save you but you. Seek your own land. You young and a woman and there's serious limitation in both, but you are a person, too. Don't let Lenore or some trifling boyfriend and certainly no devil doctor decide who you are. That's slavery. Somewhere inside you is that free person I'm talking about. Locate her and let her do some good in the world."[53]

Losses Are Often Hidden

If you're hesitant about giving up on a goal that isn't congruent with you, consider the cost of lost opportunities and mismanaged resources.

I started working on a digital product that would cover certain problems I couldn't address effectively in my books. I procrastinated on this project from the start. I realized that I was wasting my time and energy. Instead of working on a project that clearly didn't play off of my strengths, I could have directed more resources toward writing new books.

When I gave up on this project, I refocused my efforts to writing books. If I had continued to work on the project, the quality of my books would have suffered. In the end, I would have lost more than I would have gained.

In everything you do, there are always hidden costs of lost opportunities and mismanaged resources. If you had a job paying you $20 per hour that forced you to do things you hate and I told you there's a job paying $200 per hour that doesn't come with any of those drawbacks — all other things being equal — would you stick to your current job?

Working on a goal that is incongruent with you makes you lose twice: first, by causing you unnecessary suffering, and second, by making you lose opportunities in which you would generate better results with less effort.

If you still feel that you need permission to give up on something you hate, there you go:

I hereby give you my permission to give up — Martin

Don't waste your life pursuing something that turns your life into a nightmare. You'll find another way to reach your objectives that won't involve so much suffering.

GIVE UP IF IT ISN'T CONGRUENT WITH YOU: QUICK RECAP

1. If you're chasing something only because society tells you to do so — as in the case of going to the college or working in a job you hate — you're wasting resources that you could have spent on something more aligned with your personality and outlook on life.

2. If you associate your goal primarily (or even worse — exclusively) with daily negative emotions, you should give up, as the objective is clearly not congruent with your personality.

3. Working on the wrong goal doesn't just make you lose the time and energy invested in pursuing the objective itself. It also costs you in lost opportunities and mismanaged resources.

Chapter 23: Give Up If You Won't Achieve the Level of Performance or Achievement You Want

When setting a goal, define what level of performance of achievement you want to reach to feel satisfied with your efforts. If after a *realistic* period of time (remember the false hope syndrome?), your performance or achievement leaves a lot to be desired, perhaps you should give up.

"Reasonable" and "realistic" are key words here. It wouldn't be reasonable to give up on your goal of becoming a successful entrepreneur if it had only been 3 months after launching your first business. Realistically, achieving this goal takes years for most people.

Also, don't assume that you have to be the best in the world in everything you do.

Obviously, if you want to become a neurosurgeon, you'd better strive to be the best neurosurgeon in the world. You surely wouldn't want a neurosurgeon who merely wants to be "okay" at his job perform surgery on your brain!

However, if your goal isn't literally a matter of life or death for other people, you don't need to become the best in the world.

You don't need to become a billionaire to live a comfortable lifestyle. You don't need to become the fittest person in the world to be healthy and in good shape. You don't need to write like Stephen King to become a bestselling author with devoted readers.

I'll never become a world-class rock climber, but it's not important to me. I don't need the stress and dedication required to become a world-class athlete. As long as I keep improving, I'll feel good with my performance.

When I started taking tennis classes, I wanted to become an average player who could at least keep up with other casual players within a year.

A year after taking two to three classes a week, I was still losing against a friend who had played tennis no more than 10-15 times in his entire life. I realized I had an exceptional talent for being an extremely bad tennis player, so I gave up. I'm sure that even if I were to continue taking classes, I'd still remain an extremely untalented player.

Please note that sometimes progress doesn't happen for a long time, and then everything changes virtually overnight. You need to account for this fact before you decide to forgo your efforts.

I wanted to quit the self-publishing industry because I thought that I wouldn't be able to go past a certain income level. I persevered, and in the end, I did go past the level I thought wasn't possible to cross. It turned out that I didn't account for the fact that all it takes to break the financial ceiling is to release one bestseller — and with several releases a year, I had a fair chance of doing so.

Ultimately, the decision to give up or keep going when you're not satisfied with your results is a matter of managing your expectations.

If you're fine with lowering your expectations, don't give up. If you can't or don't want to accept lower standards, give up and find something else you can be good at.

GIVE UP IF YOU WON'T ACHIEVE THE LEVEL OF PERFORMANCE OR ACHIEVEMENT YOU WANT: QUICK RECAP

1. If you're unsatisfied with your results after a reasonable amount of time and other resources invested in your goal and don't see any possibilities for improvement, maybe you should find something else you'd be better at.

2. The decision to give up or keep going when you aren't satisfied with your results comes down to managing your expectations. If you can lower your expectations and still feel good, keep going. If you refuse to accept lower standards, it's better to give up.

Chapter 24: Give Up If You Only Keep Going Because of Sunk Costs

In economics and business, a sunk cost is a cost you've already incurred that you can't recover.

If you buy a non-refundable movie ticket, it's a sunk cost. If you no longer want to see the movie, a logical choice would be not to go to the theater. If you were to go, you'd suffer twice: by losing money spent on the ticket and wasting time you could have spent doing something more enjoyable than watching a movie that doesn't interest you. If you chose to cut your losses, you'd only lose the money spent on the unwanted movie ticket.

It's clear that you shouldn't go. Yet, many people irrationally choose the wrong decision. It's because of the sunk cost fallacy: the more you invest in something, the harder it is to cut your losses and quit. Another reason is loss aversion — a tendency to prefer avoiding losses more than acquiring equivalent gains.

A person would go see a movie they don't want to watch because they don't want to "waste" the ticket. They'd rather waste two hours on a boring movie and fool themselves into thinking that they didn't lose money on the ticket than lose the money spent on the ticket and gain two hours to do something more enjoyable.

According to some studies, losses produce twice the psychological effect than gains do.[54] This means that you'd work harder to avoid losses than score wins. When coupled with the sunk cost fallacy, you have a recipe for mindless persistence when the only rational decision should be to cut your losses and move on. Monitor your behavior and stop investing further resources in any endeavors where your only motivation is to avoid losses that are in fact sunk costs that you can't recover.

I shared with you a story in which I hired a business consultant. When I realized that this collaboration wouldn't work out for me, I quit. Yes, I lost a substantial amount of money, time, and energy. However, if I were to continue, the amount of lost money, time and energy would only increase. Persistence is useless if it leads to waste.

If the only reason why you're working on a goal is because you've already invested so much into it, don't delude yourself; you're throwing good money after bad. Think of your prior losses as the cost of learning. It's time to conclude your education. Quit, reflect, and move on.

GIVE UP IF YOU KEEP GOING ONLY BECAUSE OF SUNK COSTS: QUICK RECAP

1. Persistence is good as long as you care about your objective. If you're pursuing your goal simply because of sunk costs — costs you've already incurred that you can't get back — you should give up.

2. Consider your losses the cost of learning. When it no longer makes sense to pursue your goal, accept that what you've lost was in fact an investment in your education, and it's now time to conclude it.

Chapter 25: Give Up If You're Constantly Playing Catch-Up

If you constantly fall behind with your goal, perhaps the goal you're pursuing isn't that important to you or you need to give up on other goals to make time for this objective.

If you can't make time for your goal but you find time to do other things, it signals that your motivation isn't strong enough or that your objective is no longer a priority for you. If you'd like to work on your goal, but other things constantly distract you, you need to give up on those things to make time for your key goal.

We've already talked about the ineffectiveness of spreading yourself too thin. Just as trying to do several things at once reduces your performance, so does chasing too many goals.

Think of it as growing bonsai trees. If you have a hundred trees and your friend Jane has one, who's going to have more beautiful trees? You, (constantly moving from one tree to another and then rushing back to the previous one, only to have to attend to the other one again) or Jane, who has all the time and focus in the world to make her single tree perfect?

I'm not advocating that you should give up on everything. It isn't realistic or sensible to forego your family obligations, your job, and your health to focus on a single goal. However, if you're working on several "priority" goals at once, you'll be unlikely to treat them all as true priorities. A priority is a thing that is regarded as more important than another. You don't have true priorities if you have an endless list of priorities.

Playing catch-up is an obvious sign that your attention is spread too thin. Things won't change unless you give up on something. It's your choice: multiple goals and mediocre performance or few goals and excellence.

GIVE UP IF YOU'RE CONSTANTLY PLAYING CATCH-UP: QUICK RECAP

1. If you're constantly playing catch-up with your goal, it indicates that it isn't a priority to you or that you have too much on your plate. If you can find time for other things, but rarely for your supposedly important goal, perhaps you no longer care about the goal as you used to and it might be better to give up.

2. You'll maximize your results if you forego some of the less important goals and focus more on your key objective. In the end, you'll need to choose between multiple goals and mediocre performance or few goals and excellence.

Epilogue

Throughout his career, legendary baseball player Babe Ruth set the record for the most home runs in a season — 714 — while also striking out more than any other player in Major League Baseball — 1,330 times. As he was quoted to say, "Never let the fear of striking out keep you from playing the game."[55] Despite failing almost two times more than he succeeded, he became a legendary player known not for his fiascos, but for his triumphs.

He described his philosophy as follows: "How to hit home runs: I swing as hard as I can, and I try to swing right through the ball... The harder you grip the bat, the more you can swing it through the ball, and the farther the ball will go. I swing big, with everything I've got. I hit big or I miss big. I like to live as big as I can."[56]

You, too, can live as big as you can — if only you change your attitude about failure.

Don't let this book become just another title on your shelf. Go through the exercises listed throughout the book and re-read the parts most applicable to your situation.

As a final exercise, jot down *one* action you'll take to improve your life based on what you've learned. That's right; I'm not asking you much. Do just this one thing and you'll join the minority of readers who use how-to books according to their purpose — to learn and *put into practice* what they have learned. rather than fool themselves into thinking that they've accomplished anything valuable by merely reading about it.

If you opened this book unsure about how to deal with failure constructively, I hope that by now you understand that it's you who defines what failure is and that it needn't be a source of suffering.

Just like you can use a knife for two entirely different purposes — to take somebody's life or to prepare them a healthy meal —you can either treat failure as a reason to give up and never try again or as a wise teacher that helps you adjust your direction.

The choice always remains in your hands — and so does the choice to close this book and keep on living your life as before or make some improvements and start living on the next level, which is what I wish for you from the bottom of my heart.

Download Another Book for Free

I want to thank you for buying my book and offer you another book (just as valuable as this one): *Grit: How to Keep Going When You Want to Give Up*, completely free.

Visit the link below to receive it:

http://www.profoundselfimprovement.com/failure

In *Grit*, I'll tell you exactly how to stick to your goals, using proven methods from peak performers and science.

In addition to getting *Grit*, you'll also have an opportunity to get my new books for free, enter giveaways, and receive other valuable emails from me.

Again, here's the link to sign up:

http://www.profoundselfimprovement.com/failure

Could You Help?

I'd love to hear your opinion about my book. In the world of book publishing, there are few things more valuable than honest reviews from a wide variety of readers.

Your review will help other readers find out whether my book is for them. It will also help me reach more readers by increasing the visibility of my book.

About Martin Meadows

Martin Meadows is the pen name of an author who has dedicated his life to personal growth. He constantly reinvents himself by making drastic changes in his life.

Over the years, he has regularly fasted for over 40 hours, taught himself two foreign languages, lost over 30 pounds in 12 weeks, run several businesses in various industries, took ice-cold showers and baths, lived on a small tropical island in a foreign country for several months, and wrote a 400-page novel's worth of short stories in one month.

But self-torture is not his passion. Martin likes to test his boundaries to discover how far his comfort zone goes.

His findings (based both on his personal experience and on scientific studies) help him improve his life. If you're interested in pushing your limits and learning how to become the best version of yourself, you'll love Martin's works.

You can read his books here:
http://www.amazon.com/author/martinmeadows.

© Copyright 2018 by Meadows Publishing. All rights reserved.

ISBN 978-83-952523-7-2

Reproduction in whole or in part of this publication without express written consent is strictly prohibited. The author greatly appreciates you taking the time to read his work. Please consider leaving a review wherever you bought the book, or tell your friends about it, to help us spread the word. Thank you for supporting our work.

Efforts have been made to ensure that the information in this book is accurate and complete. However, the author and the publisher do not warrant the accuracy of the information, text, and graphics contained within the book, due to the rapidly changing nature of science, research, known and unknown facts, and the Internet. The author and the publisher do not accept any responsibility for errors, omissions or contrary interpretation of the subject matter herein. This book is presented solely for motivational and informational purposes only.

References

[1] Bergsma, A. (2008). Do self-help books help? *Journal of Happiness Studies*, 9(3): 341–360. doi: 10.1007/s10902-006-9041-2.
[2] *Failure*. Retrieved April 09, 2017 from https://www.merriam-webster.com/dictionary/failure.
[3] Robbins, T. (2017, March 13). Change your words, change your life. Retrieved April 09, 2017, from https://www.tonyrobbins.com/mind-meaning/change-your-words-change-your-life/.
[4] Rosenberg, M. B. (2015). *Nonviolent Communication: A Language of Life*. Puddledancer Press; 3 edition.
[5] Wansink, B., Just, D .R., Payne, C. R., & Klinger, M. Z. (2012). Attractive names sustain increased vegetable intake in schools. *Preventive Medicine*, 55(4): 330–332. doi: 10.1016/j.ypmed.2012.07.012.
[6] Wansink, B, van Ittersum, K., & Painter, J. E. (2005). How descriptive food names bias sensory perceptions in restaurants. *Food Quality and Preference*, 16(5): 393–400. doi: 10.1016/j.foodqual.2004.06.005.
[7] *Failure*. American Heritage® Dictionary of the English Language, Fifth Edition. (2011). Retrieved April 09, 2017 from http://www.thefreedictionary.com/failure.
[8] Waitzkin, J. (2007). *The Art of Learning: A Journey in the Pursuit of Excellence*. Free Press.
[9] Mollard, A. (2017, April 1). 'This is how I'm going to die. It's so unfair': Turia Pitt's tale of survival. Retrieved April 15, 2017 from http://www.dailytelegraph.com.au/stellar/turia-pitts-incredible-recovery-from-burns-is-as-much-about-love-as-survival/news-story/ff389d8d187a60a8288b40c467598060
[10] Hadgraft, B. (2014, January 29). Turia's courageous journey. Retrieved April 15, 2017 from http://www.news.com.au/tablet/turias-courageous-journey/news-story/ecff09c409a262fc49c2b8c8db7811c4?sv=28f0165d368ec395ff802aeb112e99a9.
[11] Mollard, A. (2017, April 1). 'This is how I'm going to die. It's so unfair': Turia Pitt's tale of survival. Retrieved April 15, 2017 from http://www.dailytelegraph.com.au/stellar/turia-pitts-incredible-recovery-from-burns-is-as-much-about-love-as-survival/news-story/ff389d8d187a60a8288b40c467598060
[12] Achor, S. (2011). *The Happiness Advantage: The Seven Principles of Positive Psychology that Fuel Success and Performance at Work*. Virgin Digital.

[13] Willis, J. (2012, May 22). How to Rewire Your Burned-Out Brain: Tips from a Neurologist. Retrieved April 13, 2017 from https://www.edutopia.org/blog/teacher-burnout-neurology-judy-willis-md.
[14] Michelangelo. (n.d.). BrainyQuote.com. Retrieved April 16, 2017, from https://www.brainyquote.com/quotes/quotes/m/michelange386296.html
[15] *The Enchiridion by Epictetus*, Retrieved June 30, 2017 from http://classics.mit.edu/Epictetus/epicench.html.
[16] Polivy, J. & Herman, C. P. (2002). If at first you don't succeed. False hopes of self-change. *The American psychologist*, 57(9): 677–689. doi: 10.1037/0003-066X.57.9.677.
[17] Diamandis, P. (2017, May 19). True Breakthroughs = Crazy Ideas + Passion. Retrieved May 27, 2017 from http://www.diamandis.com/blog/true-breakthroughs-crazy-ideas-passion.
[18] Sacca, C. (2017, April 26). Hanging up my spurs. Retrieved April 27, 2017 from https://lowercasecapital.com/2017/04/26/hanging-up-my-spurs/.
[19] Ballantyne, C. (n.d.) You Have Never Thought This Way Before. Retrieved April 23, 2017 from http://www.earlytorise.com/new-way-of-thinking/.
[20] Ferriss, T. (2011). *The 4-Hour Workweek*. Ebury Digital.
[21] Rowling, J. K. The Fringe Benefits of Failure, and the Importance of Imagination [speech at the Harvard University]. Retrieved April 20, 2017 from http://news.harvard.edu/gazette/story/2008/06/text-of-j-k-rowling-speech/
[22] Poitier, S. (2008). *Life Beyond Measure: Letters to My Great-Granddaughter*. HarperCollins.
[23] Knight, P. (2016). *Shoe Dog: A Memoir by the Creator of Nike*. Scribner.
[24] Elliot, A. J., & Church, M. A. (2003). A Motivational Analysis of Defensive Pessimism and Self-Handicapping. *Journal of Personality*, 71(3): 369–396. doi: 10.1111/1467-6494.7103005.
[25] Norem, J. K. (2008). Defensive pessimism, anxiety, and the complexity of evaluating self-regulation. *Social and Personality Psychology Compass*, 2, 121–134. doi: 10.1111/j.1751-9004.2007.00053.x.
[26] Rotter, J. B. (1966). Generalized expectancies for internal versus external control of reinforcement. *Psychological Monographs: General & Applied*, 80(1): 1–28. doi: 10.1037/h0092976.
[27] Paul, J. & Moynihan, B. (2014). *What I Learned Losing A Million Dollars*. Seneca and Marcus LLC.
[28] Paul, J. & Moynihan, B. (2014). *What I Learned Losing A Million Dollars*. Seneca and Marcus LLC.
[29] See https://foreverjobless.com/ev-millionaires-math/ for a great explanation of this concept and its application beyond poker.

[30] Merritt, A. C., Effron, D. A., & Monin, B. (2010). *Moral Self-Licensing: When Being Good Frees Us to Be Bad. Social and Personality Psychology Compass, 4(5): 344–357. doi: 10.1111/j.1751-9004.2010.00263.x.*
[31] Willbond, S. M., Laviolette, M. A., Duval, K. & Doucet, E. (2010). Normal weight men and women overestimate exercise energy expenditure. *The Journal of Sports Medicine and Physical Fitness*, 50(4): 377–384. doi: n/a. PMID: 21178922.
[32] *Tahnee DVD*. Robbins Madanes Film. October 1, 2004.
[33] 1997 June 1, Chicago Tribune, "Advice, Like Youth, Probably Just Wasted on the Young" by Mary Schmich, Page 4C, Chicago, Illinois. (ProQuest)
[34] Ilgner, A. (2003). *The Rock Warrior's Way: Mental Training For Climbers.* Desiderata Institute.
[35] Benassi, V. A., Sweeney, P. D., & Dufour, C. L. (1988). Is there a relation between locus of control orientation and depression? *Journal of Abnormal Psychology*, 97(3): 357–367. doi:10.1037/0021-843x.97.3.357.
[36] Seligman, M. E. P. (1972). Learned helplessness. *Annual Review of Medicine*, 23(1): 407–412. doi: 10.1146/annurev.me.23.020172.002203.
[37] *Altmaier, E.M. & Happ, D.A. (1985). Coping skills training's immunization effects against learned helplessness. Journal of Social and Clinical Psychology, 3: 181–189. doi: 10.1521/jscp.1985.3.2.181.*
[38] Seligman, M. E. P. (2006). *Learned Optimism: How to Change Your Mind and Your Life*. 2nd Edition..
[39] Kubler-Ross, E., & Kessler, D. (2005). *On Grief and Grieving: Finding the Meaning of Grief Through the Five Stages of Loss*. Scribner.
[40] Kiss, J. (2014, March 9). 23andMe admits FDA order 'significantly slowed up' new customers. Retrieved May 30, 2017 from https://www.theguardian.com/technology/2014/mar/09/google-23andme-anne-wojcicki-genetics-healthcare-dna.
[41] Miller, C. C. (2013, November 11). For $99, Eliminating the Mystery of Pandora's Genetic Box. Retrieved May 30, 2017 from https://dealbook.nytimes.com/2013/11/11/for-99-eliminating-the-mystery-of-pandoras-genetic-box/?_r=0.
[42] Warren, R., Smeets, E., & Neff, K. (2016). Self-criticism and self-compassion: Risk and resilience. *Current Psychiatry*, 15(12): 18–21, 24–28, 32. doi: n/a. PDF available at http://self-compassion.org/wp-content/uploads/2016/12/Self-Criticism.pdf.
[43] Wegner, D. (1994). Ironic Processes of Mental Control. *Psychological Review*, 101(1): 34–52. doi: 10.1037//0033-295X.101.1.34.
[44] Critchell, S. (2013, June 8). Vera Wang honored for her lifetime fashion passion. Retrieved May 31, 2017 from https://www.washingtonpost.com/lifestyle/style/vera-

wang-honored-for-her-lifetime-fashion-passion/2013/06/06/32dbd932-cd2a-11e2-8845-d970ccb04497_story.html?utm_term=.259e37cd879e.
[45] Aftosmis, M. (2007, November 19). Dress for Success. Retrieved May 31, 2017 from http://www.seventeen.com/fashion/advice/a9119/vera-wang-sept06/.
[46] Mendick, R., & Bloom, B. (2016, September 10). A tale of two Ellies: how Ellie Robinson, 15, struck gold after watching her idol Ellie Simmonds swim at London 2012. Retrieved May 31, 2017 from http://www.telegraph.co.uk/news/2016/09/10/a-tale-of-two-ellies-how-ellie-robinson-15-struck-gold-after-wat/.
[47] Ellie Robinson. Retrieved May 31, 2017 from http://www.19eleven.co.uk/team/ellie-robinson/.
[48] Kagan, N. (2017, May 16). How to Create an Interesting Life with Tynan. Retrieved May 19, 2017 from http://okdork.com/create-interesting-life-tips-from-tynan/.
[49] Streitfeld, D. (1993, October 8). The Laureates's Life Song. Retrieved June 1, 2017 from https://www.washingtonpost.com/archive/lifestyle/1993/10/08/the-laureatess-life-song/10d3b79b-52f2-4685-a6dd-c57f7dde08d2/?utm_term=.6e4fa0a59dc1.
[50] Ghansah, R. K. (2015, April 8). The Radical Vision of Toni Morrison. Retrieved June 1, 2017 from https://www.nytimes.com/2015/04/12/magazine/the-radical-vision-of-toni-morrison.html.
[51] Dreifus, C. (1994, September 11). Chloe Wofford Talks About Toni Morrison. Retrieved June 2, 2017 from http://www.nytimes.com/1994/09/11/magazine/chloe-wofford-talks-about-toni-morrison.html?pagewanted=all.
[52] Als, H. (2003, October 27). Ghosts in the House. Retrieved June 2, 2017 from http://www.newyorker.com/magazine/2003/10/27/ghosts-in-the-house/.
[53] Morrison, T. (2012). *Home*. Knopf.
[54] Kahneman, D. & Tversky, A. (1992). Advances in prospect theory: Cumulative representation of uncertainty. *Journal of Risk and Uncertainty*, 5(4): 297–323. doi:10.1007/BF00122574.
[55] *Babe Ruth Quotes*, Retrieved May 28, 2017 from http://www.baberuth.com/quotes/.
[56] *Babe Ruth Quotes*, Retrieved May 28, 2017 from http://www.baberuth.com/quotes/.

Lightning Source UK Ltd.
Milton Keynes UK
UKHW040619170119
335636UK00004B/72/P